In Darkness Light Dawns:

PURPLE CROWN
PUBLISHING

Port Colborne

In Darkness Light Dawns:
Exposing Workplace Bullying
Lisa M. S. Barrow, DM
Port Colborne

Scripture quotations are taken from the Holy Bible, New Living Translation, copyright © 1996. Used by permission of Tyndale House Publishers, Inc., Wheaton, IL. All rights reserved.

Printed in the United States of America

Book design by www.KarrieRoss.com
Proofread by Terri Young
Book edited by Leona Enns

Published by Purple Crown Publishing,
Port Colborne, Ontario
Visit our website at www.purplecrownpublishing.com

ISBN 10: 0-615-31142-3

Library and Archives Canada Cataloguing in Publication

Barrow, Lisa M. S
    In darkness light dawns : exposing workplace bullying / Lisa M.S.
Barrow.

ISBN 978-0-615-31142-5

    1. Bullying in the workplace. 2. Harassment. I. Title.

HF5549.5.B84B67 2009   658.3'145   C2009-905415-9

DISCLAIMER:
The names of parties involved in
the bullying experiences have been changed.
All of the bullying incidents are true.

*In memory of my dear
father and mother,*

John Will and Lois Iona Burks;

*my sister
Elaine;*

*and my brothers
Willie, Oscar, John, Joe,
Delmonte and Zack*

Speak up for those
who cannot speak for themselves.

—PROVERBS 31:8

Contents

PART II
Understanding Workplace Bullying

Preface

The catalyst for writing this book was an email I received from Wanda, a woman who told me she was planning to commit suicide once her savings were exhausted. The mother of a 14-year-old boy, Wanda was reaching out to me in her hour of desperation. Her intent to commit suicide stemmed from bullying she'd suffered at work. Wanda could no longer deal with the abuse so she quit her job and began planning to end her life.

As Wanda and I conversed by email, my heart was deeply touched. I wanted desperately to help her but my power was limited because I had no way of locating her or establishing personal contact. A sense of urgency grew within me as I tried to convince Wanda to change her mind and seek help immediately. I prayed for her and asked God to watch over her. A few days later, I heard from Wanda and was relieved to know she was still alive.

Unfortunately, I haven't heard from Wanda since and don't know if she carried through with her plan.

What I do know is that my involvement with this troubled soul awakened in me the previously dormant passion to do something to stop workplace bullying.

As I considered the millions of employees who are bullied on the job each day, I knew I could no longer remain silent about the years of bullying I'd experienced. I knew I'd suffered what I had for such a time as this. I knew it was time to reach out to other hurting people to let them know they could have victory over their abusers and regain their lives, as I had.

If you are currently being bullied at work or have been bullied in the past, know there is a way out of the situation. You don't need to take your life in order to escape the pain.

If you are a workplace bully, know that the impact of abuse is devastating. I want you to be so convinced of this that you vow ***never to bully anyone again***.

If you are an organizational leader or politician, I ask you to listen with an open mind to my appeals for legislation and policies that protect employees from workplace bullies. You can no longer ignore the problem of workplace bullying, which contributes to the illness and death of many employees.

I wrote this book with urgency, because of my deep concern for people who are hurting. I also wrote with gratitude, because of my deep appreciation for blessings received.

To my heavenly Father, thank You for giving me the strength to endure the bullying and the opportunity to share my story. Thank You for giving me a peace that surpasses all understanding and for filling my life with hope.

To my husband George, thank you for your love and for being my voice of reason. To my editor, Leona Enns, thank you for your patience, prayers and dedication to this book. You are a remarkable person. To Terri Young, my proofreader, thank you for your insights and incredible attention to detail. To my sisters, Iona Jenkins, Maureen Coles, Earli Burks and Mary Hales, thank you for your prayers, love and words of encouragement. To my brothers, Evon Burks, Freeman Burks and Eral Burks, thank you for teaching me at a young age to stand up for myself and not to be afraid of bullies. To my dear friends, Dianne Oster, Peggy Biggar, Sue Duemo, and Loretta Vanderhoek, your constant prayers and support were instrumental in keeping me focused as I traveled this journey. To Angie Kasten, thank you for all you do to create healthier workplaces. Finally, to the many dear souls who contacted me about your bullying experiences, I thank you for your courage and willingness to share your stories.

Part I

My Workplace Bullying Story

CHAPTER 1

Welcome to My World...
And to this Book

I've stared hostility in the face. I know how it affects people emotionally, socially, mentally and physically.

I am six years old. Tears are streaming down my mother's face and horror fills her eyes as images of violence—of people being fire-hosed and brutally beaten—appear on TV. My father sits quietly as if the impact of what he is seeing has stolen his capacity to respond.

We are watching NBC news coverage during the 1960s in our humble two-story farmhouse in upstate New York. I know something awful is going on and for a few moments, worry that the same thing could happen to us. After all, aren't we the same color as the people who are being attacked?

Then I think of my friends, who are the same color as the people who are doing the attacking, and feel sure they'd never do anything like that to me.

Years later, I'm in high school, sitting at the kitchen table with my mother on a cold winter night. Her face, usually cheerful, is weary and downcast. Her eyes, often dancing, are filled with despair. I must have seen earlier signs of her pain but on this night, it cuts me to the quick, as I realize just how deep her suffering is.

She's talking with me about her work at the dress factory, where she presses dress after dress in heat that makes the sweat drip from her brow. She's not complaining about the work but expressing pain and grief about the mistreatment she's suffering at the hands of her supervisor, whose hostility toward her has worsened over the years.

From a young age, I've been keenly sensitive to injustice. Memories like these help to reveal why. Although I've never been hosed or beaten, I know the terrible destructiveness of racism, sexism and other forms of oppression. Because I've been bullied in the workplace—something I never thought would happen to me—I know in my bones, just as my mother did, what it means to be looked down upon, to be scorned, to bear the brunt of other people's rage. I've seen the damage in flesh, blood and tears that the inhumanity of people toward one another can inflict.

Just as I've been sensitive to injustice all my life, so I've vowed all my life to fight it. Today, having survived years of bullying, I stand in solidarity with all those who suffer injustice at the hands of their leaders at work, whether racism, sexism or any other brand of hatred is involved.

Bullying, the topic of this book, involves a specific form of injustice that politicians, legislators and others are finally starting to recognize as a prominent feature of workplace life: ***repetitive abusive behavior that devalues and harms other people on the job***. Bullying is also known as "psychological harassment" or "emotional abuse." A bully seeks to intimidate and torment his or her target, attempting to strip that individual of all dignity and self-esteem.

In Darkness Light Dawns: Exposing Workplace Bullying tells the story of how I was bullied in the workplace year after year, enduring mental and physical anguish, and of how I not only survived but came out stronger for the ordeal. My purposes in sharing my story are to document the impact bullying has; to encourage others who are still being bullied; to take a stand against this unacceptable violation of human dignity and worth and to put an end to bullying in the workplace. If you are suffering from any form of emotional abuse at work, know that you are not alone; millions of others worldwide are fighting the same battles with you. You have my deepest empathy and greatest respect. I hope that by reading my story, you find insights that empower you and help you persevere in the struggles you face. May you find comfort in these pages, as if I were right beside you, listening to you, understanding you, hugging you, weeping with you and praying for you, and upon my departure, passing my torch of hope into your hands.

Part I of this book, up to and including Chapter 8, is devoted entirely to my story. My bullying ordeal is universal in significance because of its commonly experienced themes: the loss of innocence in being bullied for the first time; or the desire to run away or escape; the hope of a new start and the agony of dashed hopes. The details of individual bullying stories may differ but generally speaking, what I experienced is common in workplaces worldwide.

Part II of this book provides a broader, more theoretical perspective on workplace bullying. You may be the target of such abuse; the colleague, friend or family member of someone who is being bullied; a corporate manager seeking insights into workplace dynamics that affect the bottom line; a researcher investigating workplace issues, or a politician wanting to bring about positive change. Whatever the case, Part II will lay a good foundation for you, allowing you to make informed decisions and respond with greater sensitivity and courage to bullying-related issues that arise.

Within Part II, Chapter 9 provides an in-depth description of workplace bullying, including a profile of a bully.

Chapter 10 focuses on employees who are the target of emotional abuse. It presents my own research findings on what forms of bullying such individuals experience, how the harassment affects their health and wellness, and how they respond to the abuse.

Chapter 11 provides three defining traits of bully-prone organizations and explains why they are doomed to fail in a competitive marketplace.

Chapter 12 lays out practical steps to combat bullying if you are the target of workplace abuse, from documenting each incident of harassment to seeking legal counsel if all else fails.

Chapter 13 describes the pressing need for anti-bullying laws and my role as a lobbyist for such legislation in New York State.

Chapter 14 tells a true story that demonstrates the ultimate price of bullying; it also provides closing words of encouragement and hope.

Looking back on the road marked "bullying," which I've traveled for the past 10 years, I remember the early days of shock at being emotionally abused; then the long, dark tunnel of almost relentless pain, as the harassment escalated; and finally my recent years of healing. And no, healing is not pain-free, nor does it happen overnight.

Ten years ago or so, I encountered my first bully at work and began to experience how intense the pain of being psychologically harassed can be. After months of torment, I switched jobs in efforts to escape the bully and enjoyed about a year's respite before a whole new chapter in my bullying saga began. Now it wasn't only one person who was bullying me but an entire network of people who deliberately and systematically worked to destroy my credibility and peace of mind.

Without giving too much away (more on this in later chapters), leading by intimidation was the acceptable code of conduct in this organization. I tried to fight the establishment by being considerate and compassionate in my supervisory role and by speaking up against bullying in the workplace. This was a lonely battle. It was me alone, against the entire establishment of this large organization. The more I fought against the bullying, the more the bullies tried to hurt me. But, I would not give up. I refused to let them destroy me. Instead I clung to my faith in God, my sense of dignity and the knowledge of my own worth.

My experience of being bullied spanned two jobs and almost seven years. Adding another three years for healing, my "Course in Bullying Survival," spanned a full decade. I could not have borne it, if I had known in advance that I'd spend 10 years dealing with bullying. I would not have chosen to go into that dark place where bullying lurked in all its ugly manifestations: insidious, covert sabotage; pervasive negativity; deceit; rumors; lies; in your face hostility; mental and emotional abuse. Yet here I am, by the grace of God. My wounds are healed, my sense of humor is intact and love, not bitterness remains the guiding principle of my life. I've stared hostility in the face. I know how it affects people emotionally, socially, mentally and physically. I have a new understanding of how much people can achieve … and how much pain they can inflict. I'm stronger because of what I've survived. I'm also more hopeful. I believe that by working together and not giving up, we will eradicate psychological harassment one day.

I have also learned to trust God more and to become more passionate about two things: reaching out to people who are oppressed and standing up against oppression. These two passions are the twin purposes of my life. God has gifted me with the pain and suffering of being bullied to bring me more deeply in touch with my life's calling, so that I am both more able and more inspired to do what I was created to do: bring workplace bullying out of the darkness and into the light.

This brings me to you, dear reader, especially if you are being bullied. More words from my heart to you are in Chapter 8. Practical tips for you are in Chapter 12. But right now, I urge you to seek the support of family and friends as much as possible. I want you to remind yourself often of just how valuable you are. Seek the support of those you know will reinforce this truth. Even if you feel you cannot make it through one more day of work, draw on the courage within yourself and say: "I am loved. I matter. I will not be defeated. I will be victorious. I will survive this situation. I will not let anyone steal my hope." Print this out, copy it and post it in as many places as you like, where you will see it several times each day. Post it on your bathroom mirror, your refrigerator door, the dashboard of your car, your computer screen. Carry it in your wallet. Read it over and over again. Every time you read these words, believe them fully. Make them your mantra. Recite them to yourself whenever you need courage.

We are in this together. In writing to you, I'm also writing to myself. I'm encouraging myself to remain hopeful. I'm encouraging myself to keep speaking up against bullying in the workplace, no matter how deeply entrenched it might be within corporations, and no matter how strong a particular bully or network of bullies might appear.

Remember, we may not always understand why bad things happen to us but we can always choose to be hopeful. We can choose not to succumb to the bullying. We can uphold the value of all people, even those who have hurt us.

As fellow human beings, we must stand alongside one another and work together for a better world. When we come together, sharing a common vision, we can achieve the unimaginable. For such a time as this, God has created us. For such a time as this, God has called each of us to light a candle of hope amidst the gloom. Together we will overcome the darkness with our light.

CHAPTER 2

Innocence Lost: My First Bully Appears

I had no conceptual framework to help me describe and process what was happening to me, only a deep pain that—like my mother's pain—became more intense as time went by.

By way of background to my bullying story, let me start by saying this: Work is more than just a way of making money for me. It's an integral part of my identity—a life theme, if you will—and a prominent aspect of my heritage. For generations my people have shouldered humble responsibilities with great dignity, embracing the value and nobility of honest labor.

I have great pride in being able to say that I have come from generations of people who have worked, and worked hard. In my veins is the blood of people who picked cotton and peanuts more than a century ago in the Deep South and, only a generation ago, green beans by the acre in upstate New York.

My great grandfather Friday Davis was a turpentine worker in the Deep South. Along with many other black Americans during the late 1800s and early 1900s, he spent many hours laboriously scraping the base of pine trees in order to extract crude turpentine, which was then taken to the still for processing.

Friday Davis instilled in his daughter—my maternal grandmother, Laura Davis Boykin who toiled alongside him—the importance of working hard.

In turn, my maternal grandmother instilled the same values in my mother, the late Lois Iona Burks. My grandmother would say to my mother, "Lois, never sit down and let someone wait on you. You always do what you can. You are to work, be independent, earn your living, be honest and live a clean life."

As I grew up in Jordanville, New York, my mother gave the same advice to me.

I say these things so you will know where I have come from and what my values are. I say these things so you will understand the depth of my conviction, when I speak about the importance of work and the respect honest labor deserves.

My mother and father moved to New York State from Alabama during the late 1940s to give their children a better chance at receiving a quality education. They were not book smart, these two brave souls from Alabama, but they had a great deal of wisdom and insight, which I always appreciated.

My father, the late John Will Burks who had the equivalent of a third-grade education, had picked cotton and peanuts as a sharecropper in Alabama and also drove tractor for various landowners. After moving to New York State, he toiled long hours as a farmer, snow-plow operator and factory worker. We grew beans and corn on our 400-acre family farm and raised pigs, chickens and cows.

I was the fourteenth of fifteen children in our family. As you can imagine, the farm was labor-intensive, demanding all the hours even our sizable family could devote to it. As a child, I played with my little brother Zack alongside fields where my dad was plowing. I remember seeing the sweat pouring from my dad's face and the dirt covering his clothes. When I was older, I helped with picking beans and corn (all those seemingly endless rows!).

If my father worked hard, my mother worked even harder—not that anyone was comparing. In addition to mothering 15 children, she helped in the fields and worked for many years as a presser at a dress factory. A woman of great faith and cheerful disposition, she never complained about her job at the dress factory even though the working conditions were oven-like and the environment oppressive. She never complained about the supervisor who mistreated her year after year, damaging her health grievously and wounding her soul.

I say these things so you will understand that I, too, learned to work, and work hard, just like the generations before me. Because of my mother's experience, I also developed a sensitivity to how people are treated at work and a passion for fighting injustice in the workplace.

Surprisingly, the abuse my mother suffered at work and the increasing pain and weariness I saw in her eyes never kept me from believing that if I worked hard and did a good job, I would be rewarded accordingly. For most of my career, in fields ranging from social services to manufacturing, this turned out to be true.

Almost without exception, my superiors and colleagues treated me with respect and appreciated me for the insights I had. With each new experience, I grew professionally and personally. With each new experience, I gained confidence. I believed I could conquer all workplace challenges and sought to demonstrate this at every opportunity.

Although I didn't recognize it for what it was at the time, my first experience of being bullied took place at an automotive manufacturing plant in Ontario.

At first, all was well. I worked as a supervisor for three years, then was transferred into the production and logistics department. I saw my new role of production scheduler as an opportunity to broaden my understanding about production processes as well as the organization as a whole. The knowledge I gained would help me compete for promotions within the company. I had dreams, big dreams of climbing the corporate ladder. But I knew I needed to pay my dues first.

Production scheduling was a high-pressure job, requiring me to liaise between production managers, suppliers and transportation companies. I had deadlines to meet, schedules to juggle and goals to achieve. Above all, the lines had to be kept running.

Each day, I managed a 200-part inventory for the rear axle assembly department. I had to ensure that production had enough parts to meet daily quotas. I also had to make sure suppliers knew what to ship to us and when to ship it.

Any interruption in production was costly, especially if an entire assembly plant was affected. At the time, the cost for shutting down an assembly plant was $1 million per day. I wanted never to be the reason for a shutdown.

When I took on my new job, I discovered several parts on order that we didn't need because we already had too many of them or they had become obsolete. Upon making this discovery, I promptly contacted the suppliers and directed them to stop shipping the parts until further notice. The suppliers were not happy but complied, allowing me to streamline our operations and eliminate needless expense.

I say these things so you will understand the optimism and passion I brought to my work. I was excited about the challenge in this new role and enjoyed making a difference within the company.

Things went well for a couple years until a new manager was assigned to the department. By this time, I had almost completed my master's degree in industrial technology at Buffalo State College. I was writing my thesis on Just-In-Time Manufacturing and seeking to apply the concept at work as opportunities arose.

The new manager (I'll call her 'Jullene') was touted as being an expert on Just-In-Time principles, a strategy designed to reduce costs by producing parts for assembly only when they are needed—not sooner, not later. I was thrilled to have Jullene on board and looked forward to learning from her and sharing some of my research with her. I was eager to show her that we were of like mind when it came to implementing Just-In-Time. I quickly learned, however, that Jullene wasn't interested in hearing what I had to say. It didn't take me long to figure out the reason: she wasn't very knowledgeable about Just-In-Time at all!

Jullene envied me, I came to realize, but would never admit it. She felt intimidated by me, I came to realize, but would never show it except by trying to keep me in my place. After all, how could someone at my level—a mere scheduler, in her eyes—have more knowledge and understanding of Just-In-Time than she did?

Naively, I had assumed that any knowledge I acquired could only be an asset in my career. I didn't realize it could also introduce pitfalls in the form of negative attitudes and behaviors displayed toward me. I didn't realize it could trigger bullying instincts in a manager I had approached in good faith, with an open heart and mind, and had fully expected to support.

That very openness on my part—that innocent willingness to reach out and share knowledge and ideas, just as I'd been taught to do—made her negative attitudes and behaviors toward me that much more difficult to bear. Not having researched workplace bullying at the time, I had no conceptual framework to help me describe and process what was happening to me, only a deep pain that—like my mother's pain—became more intense as time went by.

I had worked, and worked hard. I had shown respect for my manager and colleagues and expressed my willingness and eagerness to contribute my best knowledge and skills to the team. Yet I had unwittingly awakened in Jullene a desire to torment me—to make life miserable for me, to stand in the way of my success and attempt to destroy me. This desire may not have been entirely conscious on her part but that did not lessen its powerful impact on me.

I had once looked forward to going to work but now work became grievous to me, a place of great suffering, bringing weight to my shoulders and an ache to my heart.

"How will I survive?" I often wondered, just as countless oppressed workers around the world still do. "How will I make it through even one more day?"

CHAPTER 3

Anatomy of a Disaster: My First Bullying Experience Up Close

Bullies love to create what I call "webs of manipulation" in order to inflict harm on the targets of their wrath.

Bullying can seem abstract until it breathes its foul breath in your face, whacks you on the side of the head and sucks the life from your bones, leaving you staggering with its sheer cruelty and injustice. Bullying threatens your health and your livelihood because it makes work unbearable and puts your ability to perform in jeopardy. You cannot fully understand what a formidable enemy bullying is until you meet this beast face-to-face.

You may have considered yourself immune to bullying because of your consistent goodwill toward people, your belief in the essential goodness of humanity or your overall strength and competence. Then one day a bully comes knocking at your door and your whole life changes.

So it was with me. As mentioned in the previous chapter, my upbringing had given me a positive outlook on life and a great capacity for hard work, but it had not prepared me for the possibility that I would ever bear the brunt of bullying—especially not with envy as the cause.

My parents had taught me to be happy for people when they were successful. Instead of envying them, I was to learn from them and work hard for what I wanted.

From a young age, I internalized this lesson. If someone received a promotion, I extended my best wishes. If someone was recognized for doing a good job, I was happy for him. If I lost out to a competitor, I congratulated the person. It never occurred to me to sabotage anyone else's good fortune.

Coming from this background, I found it unacceptable and ultimately unfathomable that Jullene would behave toward me the way she did. I knew intellectually that her negativity stemmed from envy but my emotions still churned with the injustice of being treated in a way I did not deserve and would never treat anyone else.

If I were in her position, I wouldn't have felt even the slightest pang of envy—I'd be too busy dreaming up ideas for collaboration. I'd be thrilled to have someone on board who was interested in a topic that also interested me. I'd be eager to forge ahead, leveraging our pooled expertise to really make a difference in the organization.

The first time I met Jullene was during a boardroom meeting. She seemed friendly and energetic and at the time, I had no reason to doubt the authenticity of her goodwill. I soon confided in her, sharing my career ambitions. She seemed happy to mentor me and promised to do what she could to help me advance in my career.

But then things changed. Perhaps Jullene's intentions toward me were secretly hostile from the start and she drew me into her confidence only to gather information she would later use against me. This is a common tactic among bullies. Or perhaps she developed antagonistic feelings toward me as I began to expose her "false front" as a Just-In-Time expert and my own knowledge, skills and initiative were revealed. Either way, she became increasingly negative toward me as time went by.

The bullying was subtle at first, as it often is. Jullene started by questioning my work, honing in on tiny flaws in my performance and finding fault and criticizing me at every opportunity. At first I accepted this as her way of challenging me to improve. But I began to have misgivings when my performance reviews, until then very good, started to suffer.

Fortunately for my sanity, I had enough self-awareness and inner strength to know that neither my work performance nor my dedication to my job had changed. The difference was simply this: Instead of viewing my efforts with objective eyes as my previous manager had done, Jullene viewed them with critical eyes. No matter what I did, it would never be good enough. The harder

I tried to meet her standards, the higher she set the bar. I was doing a good job, yet I was treated like an incompetent failure.

I am patient by nature. I like to talk about issues in hopes of resolving them. I decided to discuss the situation with Jullene when the time was right. I approached her in order to get the issues on the table. Perhaps talking with her would help, I thought. Perhaps she would help me understand something I was missing. Perhaps she would clarify her mentoring approach.

But instead of listening to me and doing her part to help bridge the impasse, she became defensive and irate, acting as if I were in the wrong for even approaching her. Jullene was quick to let me know she was disappointed in me because I was unable to meet her demands, even though she was constantly changing the rules. She challenged my decisions on a regular basis and sought to micro-manage me. Jullene relied on micro-managing as a way of controlling me and keeping me in my place. Her message was loud and clear; in her eyes I was incompetent.... period. Nothing I did or said would change her mind. Only later did I learn that this, too, is classic behavior for bullies. They hate being confronted because confrontation undermines the power they believe they possess.

Bullies love to create what I call "webs of manipulation" in order to inflict harm on the targets of their wrath. Rather than asking people outright to join them in destroying someone, they plant seeds of negativity in people's minds, causing them to question a target's motives and abilities.

Jullene shared her negative opinions about me with other leaders within the company. This influenced them in subtle and not-so-subtle ways to shun me and withhold promotional opportunities. Bullies excel at this kind of behavior, known as "mobbing" —i.e., getting a whole group of people to participate in bullying someone without overtly stating the agenda. (They are not likely to say, "Hi, I'm Jullene, let's all gang up on Lisa.") According to the Psychological Harassment Information Association, mobbing is nothing less than "a collective form of psychological violence," a "way of destroying a person without using any physical means."

The insidious webs of manipulation that bullies create can even destroy friendships, so that two people who once trusted each other now stand at a distance, wary and aloof. In my case, the manipulative power of bullying destroyed a friendship I had developed with 'Sharon', a co-worker. When I was hired, Sharon welcomed me to the organization and offered to show me the ropes. Our friendship blossomed until Jullene restructured the department, making Sharon my boss. The manager knew we were friends and began to pressure Sharon, who, in turn, increased her pressure on me.

I had trusted Sharon but as she became more and more critical of me, I began to question her motives and our relationship became strained. After a few months of working under her, I was a nervous wreck and my performance had begun to slip. The more I tried to achieve the standards she set, the more I seemed to miss the mark. This caused me a great deal of anxiety because I prided myself on being a good worker and doing things right the first time. This is the point when I no longer looked forward to going to work. I began dreading my job. The idea of quitting was a sweet daydream that seemed more and more appealing to me as the days went by.

I had developed many positive relationships with co-workers I would miss if I left. But Jullene's efforts to discredit me created a cloud of negativity that overshadowed even my most positive dealings at work.

Two factors moved me inexorably in the direction of leaving: 1) Realizing that my manager would never promote me, stalling the career momentum I had worked so hard to create; and 2) Realizing that my friendship had become adversarial because of the web of manipulation my manager had spun. Did Sharon turn on me intentionally? Maybe, maybe not. But it was clear she'd begun seeing me through my manager's eyes. My heart was broken because of the shift in my friend's actions and attitudes toward me, and because of the discrepancy between what she said to me in private and what her actions revealed.

With all of these things weighing heavily upon my mind, I began searching for ways to cut ties with this organization. I wanted to start fresh in an environment where I would have the chance to prove myself on my own merits. Eventually I landed a job at one of the company's major competitors.

On my last day of work, I said goodbye to everyone, straddled my purple Harley, put on my chrome helmet, fired up the engine and cruised out of the parking lot with two of my biker friends beside me. The hulking grey building where I had spent so many unhappy days shrank ever smaller in my rear view mirror until it disappeared entirely, as if erased from my horizon once and for all. I felt tremendous sadness coupled with relief and anticipation as I rode down the highway into my future. I had no way of knowing what I'd be riding into next.

CHAPTER 4

New Job, New Start...
Or Same Old But Worse?

The aggression hit the core of my being, unsettling me a great deal. I felt violated and suddenly unsafe in my surroundings.

My new workplace turned out to be even more oppressive than the one I'd left behind—but that's getting ahead of the story! For close to a year, all was well. Each day I drove to my new job in upstate New York and rejoiced at not having to face Jullene—the bully who had tormented me.

Looking back, I can see clues that might have alerted me to the trouble zone I was entering. In stark contrast to the glowing corporate picture my interviewers had painted, the work environment deep inside the plant was grim and dreary. Leaders routinely screamed at employees. Employees followed suit by antagonizing one another. For example, one day I observed Jim, a supervisor, screaming at Mac, an employee. Jim was angry because the automatic guiding vehicles weren't getting to the production line fast enough, causing the line to go down. Instead of asking Mac to explain what had gone wrong, Jim jumped from his personnel carrier, ran over to Mac and began cursing at him.

The profanity that spewed from Jim's mouth was unbelievable. He stood inches from Mac's face, screaming at him. Veins were popping in Jim's neck. His arms were flailing and his face was flushed. He couldn't control his saliva, which was spraying onto Mac's face.

Visibly shaken and embarrassed, Mac tried to explain to Jim what had happened but his supervisor wasn't interested in hearing anything he had to say. Instead, Jim continued to berate Mac and threatened to discipline him, then hopped on his personnel carrier and sped away.

I watched as Mac stood quietly, tears welling up in his eyes. His pride had been viciously attacked. As he struggled to compose himself, I approached him and asked if he was ok. He nodded. I told him that he didn't have to put up with such behavior and that it should be reported. He tried to pretend the incident didn't bother him, stating that nothing would be done and besides, Jim always acted this way towards him.

I told Mac I'd report the incident to HR. He begged me not to because the repercussions would be unbearable but I decided to do so anyway because injustice had occurred and I felt it had to be brought to light.

To the best of my knowledge, no action was taken to address the issue. One more bully had gotten away with abuse. One more target had suffered in silence, discounting and rationalizing the damage that had been caused.

The 30-or-so production line employees I supervised were withdrawn and zombie-like, with a deeply ingrained, experience-based suspicion of supervisors and management. Dressed in identical blue coveralls, these downtrodden, weary souls worked like robots on lines that assembled car doors. Every few seconds, heavy presses would hit thin pieces of sheet metal with a loud bang. With each bang, you could feel the vibration and see the impression created on the metal. Meanwhile, the employees were also being shaped. As surely as a press molds metal, each angry tirade was molding their attitudes and behaviors.

All of this disturbed me but I found focus and purpose in seeking to improve employee morale, which I knew would lead to improved performance. The initial wariness of the employees toward me gave way to trust as they began to see that I was truly committed to creating a more positive work environment. It took about three months of consistently dealing with them in affirming, respectful ways before the walls of hostility began to crumble. But once they did, what a difference! The employees became more open toward me but more importantly, they began showing respect for one another. Instead of fighting amongst each other, they began collaborating in order to achieve better results as a team.

Also on a positive note, a friendly competition began to develop between employees on my production line, which assembled doors for mid-sized cars, and a related group of employees who assembled doors for police cars. To my delight, 'Wendy', the supervisor who ran that production line valued employees and sought to improve workplace morale as much as I did. The two of us challenged each other daily to see which employees could produce the most. At the end of the shift, the winning supervisor would receive a cool, refreshing can of pop from one of our managers who took an interest in our game. Occasionally, he'd call to remind one of us that the other was ahead in production.

Because it was all in fun, the competition brought spice to our days while also fostering a positive atmosphere among our employees. In the midst of competing with each other, the employees became more committed to their jobs and more focused on achieving organizational goals. Best of all, the downtrodden, distant employees I'd first encountered began acting like human beings again. It was as if they were awakening from a deep sleep, as if they were coming back to life. I saw this awakening as a great victory. It was a victory against human oppression, a small pushing back against the night.

Yet another positive development during this time was Wendy's promotion to general supervisor. Wendy had worked for the organization for many years, originally as a production worker. Now, on top of going to work every day, Wendy was completing a master's degree in business, adding to her first master's degree in human resources. I admired Wendy's drive and ambition, especially as I, too, was pursuing both work and school in efforts to make a difference on the job and advance in my career.

Wendy's promotion from supervisor to general supervisor was especially encouraging to me because of the organization's deeply entrenched "old boys' network." This network powerfully resisted any movement toward inclusiveness. Many female employees who were well qualified for promotions never received them; yet upon hearing Wendy's news, I felt a sudden rise of hope. Surely change was in the wind. Surely I, too, would be promoted if I kept devoting myself to my career.

With all of these positive developments lifting my spirits and helping me recover from the trauma of my previous job, I was not prepared for a series of incidents that marked the beginning of the end for me at this organization. Forget being whacked on the side of the head. This was more like a beating of the soul: relentless, protracted and all the more injurious because it aggravated deep wounds that had hardly had time to heal.

The triggering incident for this unfortunate turn of things was a physical assault by Sam, a member of my team. The assault was bad enough. The fallout was far worse. Once again, I became a target of bullying at the hands of people with the power to ambush my well-being and annihilate my career.

How being physically assaulted by an employee led to being bullied by organizational leaders is one of the great ironies of my story. I forgave Sam. I did not press charges. I deferred to my manager (Hal) to decide in what action, if any, should be taken in response to the incident.

With spiritual beliefs that encourage and even command forgiveness, and with every intention of putting the incident behind me so I could press on in my career, I could not have been more conciliatory, more pacifistic in how I conducted myself after the assault. Yet Hal and others in positions of authority within the organization began to see me—the assault victim—as a troublemaker! Hal blamed me for repercussions from the assault even though I initiated none of it.

The downward spiral of events that followed the physical assault laid waste to the reputation I had built within the organization. It was as if Hal and other organizational leaders had developed complete amnesia about all of the positive contributions I had brought to the organization before the assault.

The following three chapters flesh out in detail what happened after the assault. For now, I will simply describe the assault, which took place not long after Wendy's promotion, after I'd been with the organization for close to a year.

When the incident occurred, I'd recently been moved from the day shift, where I had proven myself, to the afternoon shift, so I could learn about production processes there. Although suspicious of me at first, the employees under my direction soon realized I was sincere; and once again, walls of hostility and mistrust came down. Hal, the afternoon shift manager, impressed to see employee morale and performance improve, said he'd do all he could to help get me pro-moted.

At the beginning of a shift one January afternoon, I was instructing Sam about his job assignment for that shift. Sam became agitated when I told him that he would be working in a different area than his regular area. The new area was much more demanding and Sam would be more restricted by the faster pace of the line. Sam was not happy about the job assignment. But there were no signs as to how upset Sam really was, until I found myself suspended in mid-air. My chest felt as if it were in a vice. I could barely breathe. Although usu-ally friendly, Sam seemed to have 'snapped'. He had grabbed me with both arms, lifted me off the ground and was squeezing me like a boa constrictor. Thankfully, I had the presence of mind to remember that I was at work and needed to conduct myself in a professional way. I instructed Sam to put me down immediately. When he did, I told him that what he had just done was inappropriate and would not be tolerated. A colleague who was standing next to me asked Sam to explain his behavior. No answer was forthcoming but a look of remorse crossed Sam's face, as if he realized only then what he had done.

Shaken by the incident, and needing to compose myself before addressing him, I instructed Sam to go to his work area. I told him I'd deal with him later. Hal then approached me and asked what happened, as he had seen Sam lift me off the ground. He said he'd han-dle the situation and I wouldn't need to confront Sam.

The aggression hit the core of my being, unsettling me a great deal. I felt violated and suddenly unsafe in my surroundings. I was shocked because Sam had always been co-operative and helpful. I tried to figure out what I said to trigger his aggression. I had neither yelled at Sam nor treated him in a negative way. I was very polite while instructing him. I just didn't understand. I knew the situation was delicate and I'd need to be careful in how I dealt with it. How could I uphold the value of the employee while also upholding my own? What, if anything, would my manager do about the incident? For the moment, I decided to wait and see.

CHAPTER 5

The Aftermath: Bullied Once Again

Just as I believe in a forgiving God, so I believe that we as human beings need to forgive each other, recognizing that we all make mistakes and sometimes act in hurtful ways. Forgiveness is necessary for relationships to heal.

A few days after the assault, I was still shaken but no less convinced of the need to conduct myself professionally. I wanted to respond to the incident well because I knew that how I acted would set an example for other employees.

When Hal asked me how I was doing, I told him I was ok although still mystified as to the reason for the assault. As far as I was concerned, the matter was closed. Sam had been moved to a different area. Everything seemed to have settled down. I wanted to put the incident behind me and continue making a difference in the areas of employee morale and performance. That's where I wanted to devote my energy. That's where I wanted my focus to lie.

About a month after the incident, I had opportunity to talk to a friend of mine who was a senior manager at the organization. Beth was the person who'd convinced me to leave my previous employer and join this one because of the expanded career opportunities.

Due to Beth's busy schedule and frequent travel for work, we hadn't seen each other for a while. Over lunch one day, upon her return from Detroit, Beth told me she'd heard "very positive" comments about my performance and that other managers were impressed. I was happy to hear this. Beth then asked me the question that would irreversibly change the course of my career: "So, Lisa, what's been happening in your world?"

Before responding, I hesitated while the assault scene flashed through my mind. I was reluctant to say anything about it because I felt the matter was resolved. Still, the incident had indeed occurred, disrupting my world considerably, and I trusted my friend. I took a deep breath and said, "Things have been going well but I did have something strange happen to me." I then shared what had taken place.

Beth was disgusted by what she heard and wanted to know if I was ok. I assured her I was. Her disgust then turned to anger. Behavior like this cannot be tolerated, she said; senior managers should have been informed. Senior managers met daily to discuss workplace activities and concerns yet this incident had never come to light.

The more Beth considered what had happened, the angrier she became. She said she had an obligation to share this information with human resources and other senior managers including the plant manager. I assured her I was ok and nothing more needed to be done but Beth said she couldn't ignore what she'd learned. I knew she'd do the right thing but felt concerned about Sam. I wondered what would happen to him once the human resources department got involved.

A few hours later, 'Pamela', the human resources manager contacted me and asked me to come and give a statement. Pamela said she hadn't been told about the incident and that an investigation needed to take place before a decision about disciplinary action could be made. She also asked why my managers hadn't brought the issue to her attention. I suddenly realized that the proverbial "can of worms" had been opened. I didn't want to get anyone in trouble. I believed Hal had handled the situation appropriately and that he was fully aware of any actions that needed to occur. However, that wasn't the position Pamela took. I braced myself for what would happen next.

During the next two weeks, a formal investigation was conducted. Pamela told me that Hal hadn't handled the situation according to policy and would be disciplined. She said Sam's behavior was grounds for dismissal and that I could have him arrested for assault.

Concerned for Sam's welfare and aware of his 25-plus years of service with the organization, I appealed to Pamela not to fire him and stated I would not be pressing charges against him. I suggested instead that Sam receive a two-week suspension without pay, sending a message to other employees that such behavior would not be tolerated. I also suggested that any similar behavior on Sam's part in the future should lead to his termination from the company. Finally, I asked for an apology from Sam. Pamela agreed to abide by my requests. She said she'd inform Sam of the decision and ask him to apologize to me.

A few days later, in the human resource office, Sam and I met in front of Pamela. Sam was nervous and with tears in his eyes, started apologizing to me as soon as he entered the room. Sam was clearly upset with himself. He said he hadn't intended to harm or offend me. Sam had five daughters and said he'd be angry if anyone treated them the way he'd treated me.

Seeing Sam's distress, I reached out my hand and told him I forgave him and looked forward to continuing to work with him. Relief washed over his face as he realized the magnitude of the calamity that had been averted. I'd protected him from losing his job and relieved him from the burden of guilt he felt.

Just as I believe in a forgiving God, so I believe that we as human beings need to forgive each other, recognizing that we all make mistakes and sometimes act in hurtful ways. Forgiveness is necessary for relationships to heal. I forgave Sam for his sake and mine.

Forgiving Sam wasn't necessarily easy but at least the situation was clear-cut: I could resolve it by choosing to forgive. Dealing with Hal's wrath was much more difficult. As a penalty for failing to follow corporate policy, Hal was suspended for one week. I knew in my heart that our relationship would change forever upon his return. I was right. When he returned to work, he was clearly angry with me even though I had nothing to do with the decision to discipline him. I had neither questioned nor reported his way of dealing with the situation and neither intended nor wanted to get him into trouble. I only wanted to do my job, protect myself and let others know I would not tolerate abuse.

Hal's anger toward me was contagious among all of the managers, spreading like a virus that would not be contained. His anger was diffuse, free floating and for the most part not expressed toward me in words, yet what power it had within the organization! Inflamed by Hal's anger, a whole new set of bullies assembled their ranks against me. Together they were strong as steel, unswerving in their determination to destroy me.

From that point on, all of my managers branded me as a troublemaker, as someone who had to be ousted from the organization at all costs. I'd built a reputation for boosting employee morale and productivity, so that the areas I supervised hummed along smoothly; but now it was as if, in their eyes, I was a liability, a problem, and nothing more.

Some time later, Tom (Hal's boss and my department manager) contacted me on a Friday afternoon to inform me of a job opening in Detroit. I needed to decide right away whether to accept it, he said. The offer caught me off guard because I hadn't been with the organization for 18 months, as normally required before employees received promotions or other opportunities within the company.

I was cautiously optimistic about Detroit but concerned about the urgency. Why had the rules changed? What was really going on? I knew I couldn't decide to pull up roots and relocate to Detroit without knowing more about the job responsibilities and compensation; and, of course, without discussing the matter with my husband George.

Tom wasn't happy about it but I told him I'd give him my decision on Monday morning. Throughout the weekend, the more I thought about the offer, the more my suspicion rose and the more clearly the facts seemed to point in the direction of staying put.

George and I agreed. The compensation offered didn't warrant the move, especially with the significantly higher cost of living in Detroit. We'd be sacrificing too much for a mere $7,000 increase in annual pay. Plus, we weren't keen about living in the Detroit area.

With all these considerations, plus the pressure to relocate to Detroit in only two weeks, I didn't need to agonize about my decision. On Monday morning, I thanked Tom for the offer and said I'd have to decline it. The outrage on Tom's face expressed more clearly than words ever could: "How dare you turn down this job?"

My managers saw my decision as confirmation that I wasn't a team player. Yet all I did was withstand their pressure to relocate. All I did was weigh the pros and cons of moving, just as any responsible, thinking person would do. Patient and optimistic by nature, I knew other opportunities would come my way. Or would they?

Punished and Persecuted: How Escalated Bullying Destroyed My Career

To me, having my character and reputation attacked and being powerless to change the tide of opinions against me was workplace bullying in its most devastating form.

After the Detroit job offer, the bullying escalated to a degree I could never have imagined. Looking back, although I took the incident as a green light for me to take charge of my career, it was actually a red flag that might have alerted me to more trouble looming ahead.

The Detroit job offer was the first of many manoeuvres by the workplace bullies to get rid of me or stall my career. This chapter describes some of these strategies as they unfolded, one after the next. In addition to blocking my career progress, the bullies used other, less covert tactics that were equally, successful in wounding me, as this chapter relates.

But first, back to Detroit. Even though I'd harbored misgivings about the job offer and ended up declining it, I was resilient and optimistic enough at the time to consider my options. I'd been offered the job despite not meeting the usual requirement for 18 months of employment with the company so why shouldn't I pursue other opportunities? Surely other positions within the organization—positions more aligned with my experience, education and goals—would appear.

Serendipitously, or so it seemed at the time, a newly created position for which I was qualified did, in fact, turn up. The synchronous manufacturer position, as it was called, was also in Detroit but the pay was significantly higher than the job I'd turned down. Plus, the position was all about Just-In-Time and thus a perfect fit for me. I was excited about the opportunity to apply Just-In-Time principles in order to make production processes more efficient.

Serendipitous, too, was the fact that I'd met the vice president of the department in which the new position was created. He'd previously worked for the competition just as I had, and had visited the plant where I worked on several occasions.

A few months after leaving that company and joining this one, I emailed him to re-establish contact now that we were, once again, working for the same organization. I let him know I'd completed my master's thesis on Just-In-Time, as he'd previously expressed interest. I also conveyed that I was interested in positions that would make the most of my knowledge and experience.

When I now contacted the VP about the new position, he remembered me and arranged for me to be interviewed in Detroit, as I'd already applied for the job online. I made plans to fly to Detroit and went to tell Tom. He wasn't happy because he hadn't been informed about the application, as I assumed he would have been because the online form had required his contact information. Still, Tom reluctantly agreed I should go.

Little did I know that while I was in Detroit, Pamela, the human resources manager was upset because she hadn't been informed about the job application, either. Shortly after I returned home from the interviews, a manager in Detroit contacted me to say I couldn't be offered the position because it would be a promotion and the local human resources manager was opposed to it.

Needless to say, I had plenty of pent-up and not so pent-up emotions about this latest twist of the knife. I didn't understand why Pamela would resist my being promoted, especially because the position in question was not local but in Detroit. To save face, the manager in Detroit offered me a lateral position, with less compensation. It was similar to the position I'd already turned down and I declined it.

Disappointed and disillusioned, I laid low for a while, waiting for the 18-month mark, then resumed efforts to advance my career. Now, each time a suitable job became available, I applied for it and then personally notified my department manager.

More and more, I set my sights on positions that Tom had said months ago, even before the assault, would become available in the quality assurance department, which was responsible for making sure products met company standards. Surely, if decision makers could witness my capacity to improve employee morale, and could measure the resulting tangible gains in both productivity and quality, they'd want me in the quality assurance department. Once they were aware of my track record, as well as my experience, education and interests, how could they turn me down?

Well, they did, time and again. One by one, the quality positions that became available went to people with less education and experience than me—people who were either relatives or friends of managers. Nepotism was alive and well. When a synchronous manufacturing coordinator's position became available in the logistics department of the local plant, I had high hopes—hopes that were dashed yet again when the position went to a woman who knew nothing about synchronous manufacturing but was an acquaintance of two of the decision makers. The choice was a personal, deliberate affront and I knew it, adding to the sting.

Though being blocked from career opportunities was difficult to bear, there were many other forms of injustice, adding new layers to my torment. For example, I would receive a 1% bonus or raise when colleagues who were not performing well would receive 5-10% bonuses or raises. Colleagues would be allowed to go away for training in other states for a few days but my requests were denied even though the training was pertinent to my job. Often my colleagues would ignore me or distance themselves from me. When they had to talk to me, the conversation was forced and stilted.

On a few occasions I was yelled at in front of employees and colleagues. For example, at the beginning of a shift one of the managers began screaming at me because the production line was down. I explained to him that we didn't have stock to start the line because a quality problem had been carried over from the day shift. The situation was out of my control but the manager kept yelling at me and refused to listen to my explanation. He wanted to unleash his wrath and no one was going to stop him. After several attempts to reason with him, I walked away. I knew I had to act in a professional manner and couldn't stoop to the level of conduct he had displayed.

The employees who witnessed the incident were outraged because they knew I would never treat anyone in the way I'd just been treated. They wanted to defend me and protect me from further abuse. I thanked them for their concern and told them I would handle the situation. Once things settled down, I reported the incident to HR and asked for a meeting to be set up with the manager so we could discuss what had happened.

The bullying continued for a period of several years, and over time it became more and more overt, with more and more players involved. Some colleagues, for example, found a strange kind of pleasure in sabotaging my line. They would remove employees from my area, or instruct them to do something that caused the line to go down or the line performance to suffer. On one occasion, a maintenance supervisor removed a trained tool setter from my line and replaced him with a person from another area who didn't have a clue about the line.

When the line went down and I called for assistance, the maintenance supervisor began screaming at me and telling me I was incompetent, as if the disruption were my fault.

It wasn't my responsibility to train tool setters, it was his. He had deliberately created this incident in order to publicly humiliate me. I stood up to him and told him that if he hadn't removed the trained tool setter who knew the line, we wouldn't be in this situation. I told him that I knew he'd set me up and was trying to help get me fired. I was so angry with him I began to hyperventilate and felt chest pains. As I made my way to the medical department for assistance, the tears flowed and the tightness in my chest intensified.

Around the same time, I injured my back at work, and needed to ride a personnel carrier to get around the plant. Many times the vehicle would mysteriously disappear and I'd have to walk the concrete floors, step after painful step. Healthy coworkers zipped by me on their motorized vehicles. I was clearly limping and in discomfort but they drove right past me with no offer of help. Thank God for compassionate employees who would find my hidden vehicle or stop to pick me up.

For me, the most distressing form of bullying I experienced was having my character and reputation attacked. Colleagues who remained loyal to me told me what other managers were saying about me in my absence: that I was a s___ disturber, incompetent and not a team player. Words such as these cut me to the quick because of their dismissive nature and the power they had to influence others against me unfairly.

Working hard was in my blood and respecting others was in my veins yet I was painted as a rebel. I had made every effort to further the organization's cause yet I had been turned into an outcast. I was proud of what I'd been able to contribute yet my name was dirt. To me, having my character and reputation attacked and being powerless to change the tide of opinions against me was workplace bullying in its most devastating form.

I share all of these experiences with you so you will see how bullying can be subtle at times and flagrantly, unashamedly open at others. If you are not informed about bullying while you are being bullied, (as was true in my case) the pain and injustice can become unbearable. Although I did not consider ending my life because of workplace bullying, I have a great deal of empathy for people who have been pushed to this extreme.

Why, exactly, did all of this overt and covert bullying happen to me? To this day, I don't fully understand. I can point to things like trigger incidents, jealousies, desires for revenge, and evil inclinations in human nature. I can cobble together theories based on what people said and didn't say. I know that at least some of the managers who bullied me felt that I had too much confidence and needed "to be put in my place". But ultimately I will never know the full story because I wasn't able to see inside the heart of each person who chose, consciously or unconsciously, to contribute to the suffering I experienced during this time.

All I know for sure is that bullying over a period of several years put my physical strength and mental fortitude to the test. Those who were responsible may never have the self awareness to realize their part in this, let alone to ask for forgiveness. All I know for sure is that bullying is wrong, no matter what the setting, and I have devoted myself to fighting it.

How long would I be able to withstand the bullying at this organization? Not much longer, as the next chapter reveals.

CHAPTER 7

The End of the Line:
How I Finally Escaped the Abuse

**I knew this was the end of the abuse
and the beginning of my healing.**

What kept me going during those dark days? My faith in God. My strong support network. And a sense of being called to encourage and support fellow employees who were also being bullied. Reaching out to others was a saving grace for me because it gave me a reason to keep going to work even when work felt like a prison and my career momentum had stopped.

No matter where I turned, opportunities for reaching out were abundant. One day, for example, I found Jill standing in the hall crying after the assistant plant manager had yelled at her and threatened to fire her. I knew Jill was doing a good job but was still learning the system, as she was fairly new to her position. I told Jill I'd do what I could to help her learn the processes. I also encouraged her to keep believing in herself and not to let the Agnes, the assistant plant manager, intimidate her. Then I gave Jill a big hug and told her she'd be ok.

A single mother of two young daughters, Jill didn't feel any more hopeful at the time. But she went on to learn the processes and overcame her natural timidity in order to deal with the aggression that came her way. Often Jill would call me or stop by to let me know how things were going. Her smile was back along with her confidence and this brought joy to my heart.

Encounters like these meant a lot to me because I saw once again that I could make a difference in people's lives, if not in the overall emotional climate of the organization. Employees I supervised and even those I didn't, knew that I cared about them and respected them as human beings. The resulting bonds of mutual caring and respect were like lifelines that kept all of us afloat.

For many months I had to force myself to drive to the plant each morning. On the way, I listened to gospel songs (in particular, "The Battle Is The Lord's," sung by Yolanda Adams) in order to fortify myself for the day. Still, the time came when I could carry on no longer. Despite my faith in God, strong support network and the rewards of reaching out to others, I stumbled under the weight of too much darkness, too much pain. Despite my professional expertise, inner strength and natural resilience, I reeled with each new blow. I became less and less able to bounce back before the next blow came.

After six years with the organization, five of them abusive, I'd been driven to a very low place. I couldn't sleep. I was anxious all the time. I had crying spells and had lost pleasure in almost everything. One morning something strange happened, which forced me to see how bad things were. My alarm clock went off but I literally could not get up. My body felt glued to the bed. I was paralyzed. I simply could not move, no matter how hard I tried.

Imprisoned in my body, I felt a mounting panic. I had to go to work. What was going on? Why couldn't I get up? The paralysis lasted only a few minutes but my other symptoms of stress overload—insomnia, anxiety and depression—lasted much longer. When my doctor advised me to go on medical leave, I felt relieved. Humbling as it was, I knew I needed a break from the hostile work environment. I knew I needed time to heal.

I'd been on medical leave for almost three months when unexpectedly one day, I received a telephone call from work. Maggie in the HR department said I should come into her office the next day to set up my new job assignment. I knew something was amiss and went to work the next morning knowing it would be my last day with the organization.

As I drove to the plant on that warm, sunny day in May 2005, I felt vulnerable and apprehensive because of the hostility I was sure to face. Still, I knew God was with me. No matter what people said or did, I knew I'd be ok. When I asked God how I should respond to the person who would tell me I was terminated, the words that came to mind were these: "Thank you."

"Thank you?" I questioned God. "Is that what you want me to say to these people?" A still small voice said, "Yes."

From miles away I could see the water tower that was part of the plant. As I got closer, I could see the gray building itself and the surrounding fences. It looked like a prison. The only thing missing was the barbed wire.

How many times I'd driven this very route, at first elated to be able to work here; then, over time, discouraged and disillusioned. Today, as I entered the plant, I decided not to park in the lot for salaried employees where I usually parked but rather in the visitors' lot, which was located near the guard station. I knew that the guards had been instructed to monitor my comings and goings, as if I were a criminal. Today I chose to walk right past the guards, nodding 'hello', to make it easy for them to write down the time of my arrival.

My entrance through this door would not be visible to anyone in the offices. Maggie looked very startled when I walked into her office, appearing as if out of nowhere. Upon seeing me, she quickly told me we'd be meeting in Roger's office, the new human resources manager, so he could assign me my new job. I found this suspicious because the HR manager typically didn't get involved in routine job assignments. Still, I decided to interact in a positive way with Maggie and with other employees we encountered while on the way to Roger's office. Roger's office was dark when we arrived, which seemed odd because we were meeting there. Maggie had a strained look on her face and seemed nervous, but with my usual spunk, not waiting for her to take the lead, I walked into the room and flicked on the lights.

A strange sight met my eyes. Roger and Agnes, the assistant plant manager, were standing in front of the window with startled, embarrassed expressions on their faces. They'd been standing in the dark and looking out the window, watching for my approach! Roger's office overlooked the salaried parking lot. Having the lights turned off ensured I wouldn't see them had I parked in my usual spot and looked upwards on my way into the building.

Why would they resort to such behavior, as if I were indeed a lawbreaker and they were spies? I can only assume they'd intended to alert security upon seeing me so I could be escorted (or rather, paraded) out of the building after being terminated. This was common practice at the organization. It was a way of humiliating terminated employees, despite the professed purpose of protecting the property and other employees, should violence break out. Maggie, whose office faced the road leading to the salaried lot, was in on the plot; thus her startled look when I appeared in her office.

Now here I was in Roger's office, face to face with people who held my future in their hands. I had foiled their plan to have security guards remove me from the premises. Agnes, notorious for her bullying of many employees including me, quickly pulled herself together. Agnes said the meeting would be held in her office. As the four of us made our way next door to her office, I asked God one more time what I should say. Again, the answer was, "Thank you."

Roger had recently been transferred from Detroit to this HR department. He wasn't a bully, just someone doing his job. Once we were seated, he said without introduction or small talk: "Your services are no longer needed." I could see the group brace themselves for a negative reaction. I looked Roger directly in the eyes and said, "Thank you." Of all the reactions I could have made to Roger's statement, I think my simple "Thank you" caught them most off guard. The looks on their faces could only be described as "stunned". I stood up and left the office, quickly making my way out of the building so I wouldn't be accused of defacing company property. God had made a way for me not to be escorted out of the building like a criminal and I wasn't about to let anyone do anything else to humiliate me one last time.

As I made my way to my car, I walked down the middle of the road so everyone could see me. Along the way, a security guard approached me and asked me what had happened. I told him I was just terminated. He said the guards had been instructed to watch me, which, of course, I already knew. He said that I was a good person and a good supervisor and shouldn't have been treated that way. I thanked him for his comments, started my car and drove away.

As I drove, a heavy burden lifted from my shoulders. I knew this was the end of the abuse and the beginning of my healing.

Still, a deep sadness overcame me as I thought about the employees who were left behind. Jill, the single mother and many others like her would continue to face hostile, prison-like working conditions day after day in that place. I prayed that God would take care of them. I prayed that God would give them the strength to endure, the will and way to survive.

CHAPTER 8

From My Heart to Yours: Things to Know If You, Too, Have Been Bullied

The secrets to not becoming bitter, I believe, are to make healing a priority and to rediscover the truth of your own value and purpose.

Is there life after bullying? Yes! In this chapter, I'll tell you where my life has gone since that momentous day on which the bullying, for me, came to an abrupt end. I trust this closing chapter of my story will help keep your hope alive if you are still being bullied, or if you are recovering from a bullying experience. You'll see from my story how God brought good from bad. I hope you choose to believe that this can be true for you, too. As if I knew you, dear reader, and as if we were close friends, I'll share with you my thoughts about how to survive bullying while it's happening and how to start healing once it's past.

Let me begin with the ending to my story. Months before my termination at the automotive plant, I'd applied for a six-month consulting contract with a steel manufacturing plant in another city. The day after my termination, which was a Thursday, I received an email asking when I could start. Monday, I replied. And so it was that only days after I lost one job, I began my next one. God had already made plans for the next phase (a bridge phase, as it turned out) of my career.

The steel manufacturing company that hired me was desperate to turn its fortunes around, as it had lost market share and was struggling to avoid bankruptcy. In efforts to save the company from ruin, organizational leaders decided to train their maintenance employees in a program designed to improve processes and increase efficiency. My job was to present a 40-hour interactive workshop outlining this program to a different group of employees each week.

Having just left a workplace in which negative attitudes and behaviors were rampant, I was struck by the dominance of these same attitudes and behaviors in this environment. Ironically, for an organization seeking to better itself, the employees I taught were openly cynical and disillusioned because of their leaders' negativity. Many of the employees reported having been bullied by their bosses. The only hope they had was retirement. For now, they struggled to endure. Within the next few years, they'd escape.

Interacting with these employees gave me a glimmer of understanding as to why God had allowed me to be bullied. Because of what I'd gone through, I was able to empathize at a deep level with people in the trenches. I was able to establish rapport with them and encourage them. I felt passionate about fighting workplace oppression. I could understand very well, both intellectually and emotionally, the impact on employees and organizations when bullying is tolerated and human value is not affirmed.

Before leaving the automotive plant, I'd started teaching organizational behavior, leadership, entrepreneurship, marketing and management courses online for three universities in the U.S. I'd also written a book titled *Hope for a Healthy Workplace*, earned my Doctor of Management degree in organizational leadership and launched a consulting business, LMSB Consulting (www.lmsbconsulting.com). All of these pursuits helped me find meaning and purpose outside the plant and gave me something to build on once I was terminated and then again when the six-month contract with the steel company was complete.

I continued with the consulting business and online teaching during the six-month contract and have done so ever since, pursuing new business and online teaching opportunities along the way. As of January 2006, I've also been teaching "live" at a local university. Here, I'm privileged to interact with students face to face as I share my knowledge with them and help them discover their personal worth. As I stand in front of the classroom teaching management and entrepreneurship courses at the undergraduate level, I marvel at God's provision and rejoice in how "right" all of it feels. With a wealth of industry experience behind me, I'm able to do what I know in my heart I was born to do: teach.

Yes, there is life after bullying. Hearing this from someone who has come out better for it, not bitter, may encourage you to persevere in dealing with the struggles you face. If you are being bullied, know that God allows situations to occur in our lives for a purpose, even if it isn't always clear at the time. In my case, I needed to go through the experience of being bullied in order to help me reach out to others who are being bullied and advocate on their behalf. I also needed to learn more about trusting God—a difficult thing to do when the pain is fierce and no escape is in sight.

For me, at least, trust did not come easily. While I was being bullied, I shed many tears and pleaded with God many times to remove me from the situation. I tried to escape on my own a few times by applying for positions in other organizations but none of these jobs materialized.

When I cried out to God in despair, with cries that intensified as the pain grew worse, He never provided me with the immediate "out" I wanted. But each time I cried out to God, something would happen to let me know He'd heard me. Someone would call me or stop by to talk. All I needed was a little encouragement. All I needed was reassurance that I was doing the right thing and was going to be ok. I'd muster up the courage to endure another bullying episode and at the end of the shift, would thank God for helping me. Again and again, I learned that God was in charge and that He was taking care of me. And so my trust in God grew and continues to grow to this day.

Just as God didn't provide me with an immediate escape when I asked for it, He also didn't provide instant healing once the bullying situation was behind me. I say this in case you, too, are no longer being bullied but remain plagued by its after-effects. Know that it takes time to heal and be gentle with yourself while your recovery is under way. Your very being has been shaken. You need to regain strength and put those broken pieces of yourself together again.

For many months after being terminated, I experienced symptoms of Post Traumatic Stress Disorder, although I was never officially diagnosed. I was nervous, anxious and had flashbacks about the abuse. I had trouble concentrating and sleeping. I had an overall feeling of vulnerability. Except for going to work, I withdrew from people and stayed home. My wounds were open and fresh. I didn't want to risk getting hurt again.

Prayer, reflection and solitude were very important to me during this time. Even before having been bullied, I knew the value of withdrawing from distractions in order to pray and reflect. Something incredibly valuable and nourishing happens when we take time to quiet our hearts and listen to that still, small voice within. Time and time again, during my recovery, I retreated into my study and took solo walks and drives, allowing me to seek God's guidance and work through the turbulent emotions that were surfacing.

Reading the Bible—especially the Old Testament books of Psalms and Proverbs—also took on new importance for me during this season. Verses from Psalms, with all of their passion and raw honesty before God, helped in my emotional healing; and verses from Proverbs, with all of their wisdom about life, gave me the perspective I needed on what had happened and how to move on from here. The one thing I didn't want was to become bitter toward the people who had wronged me or cynical about humanity as a whole. I knew I was responsible for my attitudes and behaviors and wanted to make sure they were in alignment with God's commands.

Proverbs helped me to see the big picture. That's why I can say with confidence and honesty that I don't hold grudges against or ill feeling toward the bullies I encountered. If anything, I feel sorry for them and pray they'll realize one day that bullying is wrong and eventually brings harm to all parties involved, including the bully. I pray that someday they'll come to appreciate the value that all people bring to situations and to this world.

The secrets to not becoming bitter, I believe, are to make healing a priority and to rediscover the truth of your own value and purpose. Unfortunately, many people I've met have not done this. Instead they have allowed the experience of being bullied to paralyze them and suck the breath from their lives. By harboring anger and animosity toward the bullies and the organization where they were bullied, they embrace negativity. By embracing negativity, they buy into the bullies' lies—lies that say they are worthless, with nothing to contribute to this world. Lies that say life itself is mean-ingless; barren of love and pleasure. Lies that say life is a grim, empty and mutually exploitive affair.

The primary challenge for people who have bought into the lies of negativity is to consciously take time to heal: to work through their emotions and inten-tionally replace negative messages with positive ones. Once healed, they need to ponder what the negative experiences have taught them and discern how they can use what they've learned to help make the world a better place.

I've spoken about prayer, reflection, solitude, and about Bible reading as important avenues of healing in my recovery from workplace abuse. Also essential for me was the loving support of family and friends. Just as the telephone calls, emails and prayers of loved ones helped me get through the years of being bullied, giving me confidence and courage to face what I had to face, so their support helped me during those long months of healing afterward. If you are recovering from being bul-lied, I pray that people who care about you will reach out to you with words, touch and prayers, letting you know they are walking this difficult journey with you.

It's been several years now since my own ordeal. It wasn't until I started writing this book that I realized what happened to me was called bullying. It wasn't until I started writing this book that I realized how common workplace bullying is and how many people are suffer-ers. It wasn't until I started writing this book that I real-ized how far I've come in my recovery, although the scars remain as reminders of what I endured and how I've healed.

In writing this book, I'm showing you my scars. I do this in order to reveal what happens when people are bullied. If you've been bullied, I hope that seeing my scars will help you realize that your wounds, too, can heal; that, you, too, can survive bullying; that you, too, are worth a great deal; and that you, too, can choose to embrace life to the fullest. Take pleasure in what you are able to contribute and refuse to believe the lies!

When I said, "Thank you," to the person who told me I was terminated, I was saying it because God had directed me to say it. He allowed me to exit from the organization with grace and dignity, holding my head high. Today, I can still say, "Thank you." Not to the bullies for their mistreatment but for the good that has come from bad, because of God's providential care.

I thank everyone who supported me while I was being bullied and while I was recovering.

I thank God for strength, courage and healing; for love, mercy and grace.

And dear reader, I thank *you* for listening to my story. May you be blessed. May God go with you. In the midst of darkness, may light shine.

Part II

Understanding Workplace Bullying

What is Workplace Bullying?
The Big Picture

It may help you to remember that despite all of their arrogance and bravado, bullies are needy, weak and psychologically unwell.

I've shared my story of being bullied in the workplace so you will understand the depth of my passion about this cause. Now I want to step back a little in order to look at workplace bullying from a broader perspective.

Workplace bullying is *repetitive abusive behavior that devalues and harms other people on the job*. Workplace bullying is not physically violent but relies instead on the formidable weapons of hostile actions and words. It intimidates and torments the targeted individual, putting his or her self-esteem and overall health at risk.

Workplace bullying is rampant across all market sectors in Canada and the U.S., even though we pride ourselves in both countries on tolerance, civility and the high value we place on human rights. The impact of all this bullying, which continues, for the most part, unrestrained, is largely overlooked. Corporate leaders, government legislators and society as a whole must wake up to workplace bullying as the true menace it represents to our collective health, wellness and prosperity.

Who is Bullying Whom?

In the workplace as in the playground, bullying is an abuse of power. It is far more destructive than the bully realizes. It is unacceptable no matter what factors have led to it, no matter what incidents have triggered it, and no matter how weak or afraid the bully may be underneath that bold and brazen, "don't-mess-with-me" exterior.

According to research conducted by Zogby International in 2007, 60% of bullies are men, 40% of bullies are women and in most instances of bullying (57%), female bullies are targeting other females. Bullying can also involve women targeting men and men targeting either gender; yet the predominance of women targeting other women is striking.

As you might expect, most bullies are bosses but not all bosses are bullies! In most cases of bullying (72%), the bullies ranked higher than the targeted person; only in 18 % of cases were the targeted individual and the bully the same rank. Occasionally, a subordinate will bully a superior, and when this occurs, a woman is slightly more likely (10% vs. 8%) to be the aggressor than a man.

Most bullies (68%) operate alone, although female bullies are slightly more likely than their male counterparts (29% vs. 25%) to enlist the help of others in "ganging up" on their targets. Statistics such as these, all courtesy of Zogby International, suggest that bullying can strike anywhere within an organization. Anyone can stoop to harassing behavior and anyone can be the target, regardless of rank or gender.

Profile of a Bully

At first, a bully may come across as polite, amiable and even jovial. Remember Jullene? The term "wolf in sheep's clothing" comes to mind. At the outset, a bully may be winsome and engaging, seeking to win your trust. All the while, he or she is gathering information that may prove useful later in thwarting the goals and desires you've revealed.

Bullies typically possess a "Type A" personality; they are competitive and appear driven, operating as they do from a sense of urgency. This has its advantages in the workplace but the shadow side of Type A is the tendency to become frustrated and verbally abusive when things don't go according to their plan. Impatience and temper tantrums are common for Type A individuals who haven't engaged in the personal growth required to gain self-awareness, maintain emotional stability and consider situations from multiple points of view.

Because of the bully's "two-faced" nature—considerate if things are going well and abusive if not—his or her presence in an organization can cause the work environment to become tense. People feel as if they are "walking on eggshells" around the bully. They feel he or she is a "sleeping giant" who could, upon awakening, explode with rage.

Above all, bullies crave power and control, and this craving underlies much of what they do, say or fail to do and say at work. Bullies use charm and deceit to further their own ends and seem oblivious to the trail of damage they leave behind, as long as their appetites for power and control are fulfilled.

When confronted, bullies typically ramp up the hostility rather than curtail it because they feel a loss of control. The more threatened they feel, the more aggressive they become. Unfortunately, they are easily threatened because of the deep-seated insecurity they strive at all costs to hide, even from themselves.

If you've been bullied, you may find it difficult to see past the bully's shortcomings enough to feel sorry for him or her. But that is the first step in moving past bitterness toward forgiveness. It may help you to remember that despite all of their arrogance and bravado, bullies are needy, weak and psychologically unwell. They abuse their power in order to feel good about themselves. They lash out at others in order to protect themselves. They are afraid their inadequacies will be exposed. They are terrified of the emptiness inside their hearts, which they have not allowed love to reach.

What is Bullying all About?

What bullying looks like in specific terms is covered in Chapter 10, which explores in detail the experiences of people who have been bullied. For now, though, we can observe that bullying is usually top down, with the bully holding a position of authority that invests him or her with the power to reward and punish employees. The bully abuses this power by going beyond its rightful limits, believing that he or she is free to treat employees in any fashion.

As primitive as it might sound, many corporate leaders to this day believe that harsh treatment of employees is necessary because they (employees) will not perform at optimal levels without it. From what I've seen across many sectors of the marketplace, bullying is almost inevitable when this belief, conscious or preconscious, pervades a workplace environment and drives its affairs. (More on the bully-prone organization in Chapter 11.)

Compounding the problem, are complex personal issues on the bully's part. Even if an employee is performing well and the organization is doing its best to create a positive work environment, a leader who is predisposed to bullying others may bully in any case. The reasons for this are complicated, rooted as they are in the bully's personal history and temperament, but the craving for power and control is a common theme. Underlying this craving, in many cases, is insecurity— insecurity that manifests itself in jealousy, the need to release negative energy, the need to appear superior, the need to find a scapegoat, and the like.

Impact of Bullying on Targeted Individuals

With millions of people currently suffering from work-place bullying in the U.S. alone, consider the toll on targeted individuals, their family members and friends, the organizations in which bullying takes place and society as whole.

The impact on targeted individuals is easiest for me to address because I was one of them. In many ways, my experience was a textbook case. Targeted individuals typically experience severe emotional trauma, just as I did, along with diverse physical symptoms caused by stress. Distracted by bullying dramas that leave them physiologically and emotionally weakened, targeted individuals become less and less able to concentrate on tasks, hampering their performance at work. Eventually, their earning power may be reduced and ability to make a living jeopardized.

Tracey, mother of a young daughter, lost her health, job and home as a result of workplace bullying. Her pain is intense. As she writes in her blog:

> *It has been three years and six weeks since I left my job of nearly 20 years and yet I am still haunted in my dreams by the terrible four months that ended my successful career, devastated me personally and financially, and completely tore my heart open. It has had a lasting effect on my relationships....*

I awoke this morning exhausted. My eyes were puffy; my cheeks were red and swollen. I had a headache. Days like today I feel hopeless about having a better future for myself.... I spend my days working on healing my pride, ridding myself of shame, guilt and fear.

Impact of Bullying on Family and Friends

Needless to say, friends and family also suffer, as they watch their loved one reel from each new episode of bullying. But the suffering of friends and family doesn't stop there. They are robbed of the vibrant, well-rounded person the individual was before the bullying ordeal began. Spouses, children and others may not understand the full impact of bullying on their loved one and may struggle with feelings of helplessness because in fact, they don't know how to help. Over time, they may feel more and more closed out as the person gradually withdraws from life and shuts down emotionally.

Friends, especially those outside the workplace, may come to play an especially significant role during this time. Peggy was such a person in my life. While I was still working in a toxic environment, I would call her before a shift and ask her to pray for me. When I told her I had taken sick leave, she took a long, deep breath and said, "Thank you, God." As she told me later, she witnessed with growing concern my transformation from a fun-loving person and vibrant workplace leader into a shadow of my true self: someone who was quiet, isolated and guarded, with emotions of sadness and anger etched upon my face.

Thank God for family members and friends who offer their love and support to targeted individuals, and for those who love the targeted person but don't quite know what to do. Family members and friends are indirect targets of bullying. They need understanding and compassion, too.

Impact of Bullying on Organizations and Society

Some companies seek to promote a healthy workplace and still have a bully or two on staff. Other companies are negative to the core and, not surprisingly, are infested with bullies. Either way, companies pay a high price when bullying takes place within their walls. Predictably, under these circumstances, they are neither as productive nor as profitable as they would otherwise be.

Because the bullied person is less able than usual to focus on tasks, he or she is less able to contribute to the achievement of organizational goals. The loss of creative, productive hours is a huge loss for companies, especially when you consider, (as we will in Chapter 10), that bullied individuals are normally strong, competent individuals with much to offer their employers.

Another loss to organizations, and one that is often overlooked, is the fact that bullies generally fail to inspire optimal levels of productivity from all employees not only the ones targeted for abuse. Because of their ongoing negativity, bullies miss many opportunities to affirm employees and have difficulty fostering the sense of teamwork that spurs innovation and corporate growth.

Last but not least, bullying results in astronomical absenteeism, disability and litigation costs for organizations. These costs will only increase as global economic uncertainties continue, intensifying the "pressure-cooker" atmosphere that can trigger and increase bullying in the workplace.

Bullying is destructive on many levels and society as a whole is much the worse for it. Society is a connected web of people living together. How could this intricate web of relationships not be affected by something this damaging? When people are hurting to the point of despair, when families are in turmoil, when organizations are being drained of money, revenue potential and the positive energy that makes work fulfilling, society as a whole becomes ill.

Does bullying weaken our society, causing it to become more and more uncivil? Or does the increasing incivility of our society, (despite its lip service to civility), open the door to bullying? This is one of those chicken-and-egg questions we could discuss at length. Either way, we'd have to conclude that workplace bullying is both more common and more destructive than many of us have realized. Now that we know about it, shall we allow the mistreatment to continue? Shall we keep sleeping through it? I think not!

The Bullied Person: A Close-Up View

Instead of the "weak" stereotype,
when you think of a bullied person,
think intelligent, talented, easygoing,
motivated, and well liked by many
people—but not by the bully
or bullies!

Now that we've explored what bullying is all about and have a better understanding of bullies, let's take a closer look at the people most affected by bullying: the targeted individuals who suffer in anonymity each day in workplaces throughout North America and the world.

What do bullied individuals experience? How are their health and wellbeing affected? How do they respond to the bullying they face?

These were my questions when I began conducting my latest research on bullying. I couldn't find current statistics answering these questions to my satisfaction so

I decided to conduct my own study. These findings form the bulk of this chapter. First though, let's consider what bullied individuals are like and how the experience of bullying can begin in someone's life.

Profile of a Bullied Person

Without firsthand knowledge of bullying, you might assume that targeted individuals are, by definition, weak, self-doubting types with low self-esteem. You might imagine them as loners or as people who are generally disliked. You might think of them as people with oddball, extreme or eccentric personality traits. Who else would bullies target, if not the marginalized, most vulnerable people in their surroundings?

It's true that bullies are quick to exploit and adept at finding people's weak spots. It's also true that bullied individuals aren't necessarily people you'd define as weak. Before the bullying begins and often well into it, despite the onslaught of negativity they're battling, they may well be assertive, confident and self-assured, just as I was.

Instead of the "weak" stereotype, when you think of a bullied person, think intelligent, talented, easygoing, motivated, and well-liked by many people—but not by the bully or bullies!

What causes a bully to target a strong, self-confident person? Insecurity. An insecure manager (or someone in any other position) can feel threatened by such an individual, triggering the bullying instinct to manifest itself in all manner of pain-inflicting ways.

Bullied individuals vary in temperament and personality and some are less confident than others, to be sure. My point, though, remains: We must not buy into the stereotype by assuming that bullied individuals are weak, timid or self-effacing by definition. It is exactly the capacity to be assertive, to show confidence and initiative that often raises the ire of bullies, because of the deep, often unacknowledged insecurities they possess.

How Bullying Begins

In some instances, employees begin to experience bullying immediately upon entering into a working relationship with an individual. Whether the employee is new to the organization or has simply switched roles within the company, he or she may experience bullying from the outset if the new "boss" is the bullying type. For other individuals, bullying may not begin until they've been with the organization for some time and a precipitating event occurs.

A precipitating event could be of the kind that happened to me. As described in Chapter 5, Sam, an employee physically assaulted me. Hal, my manager, was disciplined for his failure to follow company policy in dealing with the incident. Hal then began bullying me out of anger at being disciplined, even though I had neither caused nor desired him to be penalized.

Another example of a precipitating event is when an employee speaks out about an incident of sexual harassment on the job or about being discriminated against due to race, ethnicity, disability, religion, gender or anything else. This can open the door to bullying even if the person has spoken up with the best of intentions and the highest levels of civility and respect.

The person may have trembled at the thought of speaking out, knowing all too well the potential consequences, and may even be known to all as a timid person, someone not inclined to make a scene. Still, if the bully perceives the employee as going against the unwritten rules of the organization, or as "rocking the boat" in any fashion, he or she may feel justified in labeling the employee a troublemaker.

Whether the bullying begins after a job change or after a precipitating event, the targeted employee may not realize at first what is going on. Something may not feel right at work. Something may seem "off." The employee may struggle to put a finger on it. But over time, as the negativity toward him or her intensifies, a moment of truth may occur: "Something is really wrong here. The situation is getting worse, not better. I'm working hard and doing my best to get along with everyone but this person is definitely on the attack. I'm being bullied. What can I do about it? How can I stop it? How will I survive?"

What Bullied People Experience

No two experiences of bullying are the same but researchers Charlotte Rayner and Helge Hoel (1997) have outlined five common categories or forms of bullying:

1. Threat to professional status (e.g., damaging the person's reputation, humiliating the person in public or accusing him or her of lack of effort).
2. Threat to personal standing (e.g., calling the person names; insulting, teasing or intimidating him or her; or devaluing the person based on age).
3. Isolation (e.g., preventing access to opportunities, deliberately withholding important information or isolating the person physically or socially).
4. Overwork (e.g., imposing undue pressure to produce work, setting impossible deadlines or making consistent and unnecessary disruptions).
5. Destabilization (e.g., failing to give credit where it is due, assigning meaningless tasks, removing responsibility or setting the person up for failure).

In conducting my research, I created a Workplace Interaction Survey encompassing each of those categories. After distributing it to 304 men and women in Canada and the U.S. and analyzing the responses, I concluded that significant numbers of people are experiencing or have experienced bullying in some form. For example, 28% of the 304 men and women admitted they had been bullied.

Threats to professional status, as addressed in the first category of bullying, were common. Of respondents, a full 46% had been publicly humiliated and embarrassed by a boss or co-worker.

Threats to personal standing were also frequent. Many (38%) of respondents were teased, 24% were targets of malicious rumors and 23% were talked to in a sarcastic way and felt "put down."

As examples of *isolation*, 31% of respondents reported being ostracized in the workplace and 28% had experienced sabotage of the work they were trying to do.

As an example of *overwork*, 20% of respondents said they'd received unreasonable deadlines, as commonly imposed by bullies in efforts to overwhelm and intimidate.

Destabilization was rampant. 50% of respondents indicated they didn't receive credit for their work and 35% said they were neither acknowledged nor rewarded for doing a good job.

How being Bullied affects Health and Wellness

My research confirms that bullying is powerfully and profoundly damaging to health and wellness.

Of respondents:
- 31% indicated that they suffered physical ailments such as fatigue, nervousness, headaches and stomach-aches on a regular basis due to mistreatment at work.
- 27% were depressed and became anxious when they thought about work or were at work.
- 32% indicated that being bullied had negatively affected their personal lives.

How Bullied People Respond

The question all of this raises is obvious: How do bullied individuals respond to being bullied? Although

20% of respondents said they sought professional help in order to deal with bullying, 8% reported reliance on smoking, recreational drugs, alcohol or other harmful activities. 11% of respondents said they had made excuses for not going to work.

What bullied individuals do in response to bullying is only one part of the story. Also critical is how they feel (e.g., helpless, powerless) and thus what they do not do (e.g., take a stand, get professional help, seek to change their circumstances).

In my study:
- 20% of respondents reported feeling helpless at work and were afraid to speak up about how they were being treated.
- 30% believed they did not have the power to change their situation at work.
- 31% did not feel valued at work.
- 22% tolerated the bullying because they were afraid of losing their jobs.

Learned Helplessness

People who fall into those last four categories have adopted a coping mechanism called "learned helplessness," which I will further address in Chapter 12. In essence, they believe they don't have control over their situation. They feel as if there is no point in trying to change it. As a result, they are likely to remain in the negative situation indefinitely. They become paralyzed and numb. Their vision is blurred. They see no way out.

They begin to blame themselves and feel that the negative situation affects everything they do.

Tragically, some individuals become so convinced the bullying will never end that they consider suicide. This was the case for 6 % of individuals who participated in my survey.

Personal Thoughts

I'm not surprised by the findings that bullying is common, the damage significant and people's capacity to respond pro-actively impaired. If anything, what surprises me is that the numbers aren't higher—and I suspect in reality they are. Perhaps people demoralized by bullying are not inclined, even in an anonymous survey, to fully reveal themselves. Perhaps some are in denial about the mistreatment, as I once was.

What we do see from the numbers is that bullying is real. Far from consisting of isolated instances here and there, it is a significant and troubling phenomenon, one that demands attention in business, government and academia alike.

As I ponder my research, one of the great paradoxes that comes to mind is how isolated bullied individuals often feel yet how much they have in common with fellow targets. Because of this shared suffering, great potential exists for mutual support through the Internet, support groups, personal conversations and the like. This book, I hope, will inspire people to reach out to each other in just these ways, filling the powerful human needs to have sensitive experiences validated, turbulent emotions recognized and individual worth affirmed. I have set up a community forum to further discuss workplace bullying.

Visit www.bulliednomore.com.

In all of my speaking and writing, the plight of bullied individuals is never far from my heart. More research on this large yet often overlooked population is needed in order to shed light on workplace bullying. It must stop. Workplace bullying takes a terrible toll on real people—people not much different from you and me.

Additional quantitative research will help bring the phenomenon of bullying into ever sharper focus. Additional qualitative research will flesh out the available statistics by describing individual experiences of being bullied—or of bullying—in an intimate way.

My story is only one of many. My research findings are only a starting point. I look forward to the light future research will shed on both my bullying story and the data presented here. Meanwhile, I'm grateful for the light scientific investigation has shed on my own path. Through my research, I discovered I'm in good company as someone who has suffered bullying. I've also become an authority—an expert, if you will—on the topic, allowing me to wrest good from bad!

The Tragedy of Tyranny: Why Bully-Prone Organizations Fail

Only when the precious humanity of employees is upheld can maximum levels of productivity be achieved.

No discussion of workplace bullying would be complete without due attention to the context in which the bullying occurs. Which leads me, of course, to talk about the workplace itself—not so much the physical place where work is done but the corporate culture of which each employee, like it or not, is part.

Ideally, the workplace is like a happy, harmonious family, with each person feeling valued and contributing to the whole. In reality, many workplaces today are more like dysfunctional families. Seething with interpersonal hostility, they miss opportunities for innovation and hemorrhage productive energy. As a result, profitability plummets and competitive edge is lost.

Without intentional, ongoing efforts to create a positive corporate culture, the emotional climate of an organization quickly deteriorates into a toxic stew of bitterness and mistrust. People who are prone to bullying behavior feel free to act out at will, oblivious to the battlefield of 'wounded soldiers' in their wake. In a negative environment, employees generally hate going to work and are profoundly disillusioned with the workplace, their bosses and one another.

"That's just how things are around here," many of them conclude. Or: "That's just how work is," if they've never experienced any other workplace but the bullying type. Seeing no choice but to keep putting up with the negativity, they keep putting in time, suffering one bad experience after the next, year after year. Some who are bullied become bullies. Eventually, both bullies and bullied individuals retire, die or suffer a stress-related illness. How sad!

Defining Traits

What defines a bully-prone organization? In what type of organization is this type of harassment most likely to occur? Let me say first of all that no market sector is immune to bullying. It happens in all sectors, from education to healthcare, from retail to manufacturing. It happens in government as well as private businesses, in large organizations as well as small. An organization may have noble aims (e.g., to serve persons with disabilities) but even this does not rule out the possibility of bullying behind the scenes.

Bully-prone organizations have at least three characteristics in common:

- *a centralized, oppressive authority structure.*
- *a focus on processes at the expense of people.*
- *a preoccupation with rules at the expense of innovation and creativity.*

If a company has offered you a job or if you are pursuing work with a particular company, you would do well to assess the organization first to determine if these characteristics are present. For example, ask current employees to share their experiences with you. Setup an appointment to tour the facilities. While on the tour, observe the interactions between leaders, managers, and employees. Look into the eyes of the employees. If the characteristics are present, you won't necessarily suffer bullying but the chances are higher. If you take the new job anyway, at least you'll know what could lie ahead!

Centralized, Oppressive Authority Structure

Let's begin with a centralized, oppressive authority structure. Authority is necessary, just as leadership is. What I mean by a centralized, oppressive authority structure is one that reserves authority for a select few. These select few individuals are like leaders in a totalitarian state. They dictate what will or won't happen in the organization. They don't seek input from employees because they don't see employees as capable—at least, not beyond the strict parameters of their job descriptions.

With a centralized, oppressive authority structure in place, information and decisions flow from the top of the organization down, seldom from the bottom up. Employees do as they're told. They aren't encouraged to share ideas or insights. They know their opinions don't count. Motivation for speaking up is scant because whether employees do speak up or don't, they know their voices will go unheard.

An organization with a centralized, oppressive authority structure is conducive to bullying because the checks and balances of less rigid, more flexible authority structures are lacking. People considered to be low on the organizational "totem pole" are all too easily forgotten, neglected and abused.

Processes Before People

Closely related to a centralized, oppressive authority structure is a focus on processes at the expense of people. Processes themselves are necessary. At various points in my career, I've been responsible for scrutinizing organizational processes in order to maximize efficiency and improve productivity. "How can we do this better?" is always a fair question to ask, and indeed, one every organization must ask and ask again as market conditions fluctuate.

The problem lies in focusing on processes *at the expense of* people because in all instances of production, even the most mechanized, the successful execution of processes relies on people. People are the cornerstone, the lifeblood, of any organization. They are not machines and must not be reduced to the processes they perform.

Let's talk a little more about machines. To a leader in a bully-prone organization, the organization itself is, in fact, a machine—at best, a "well-oiled machine." Employees, in turn, are parts of the machine. Like cogs in a wheel, their sole purpose is to ensure that the machine keeps producing, and producing efficiently.

All of this might sound benign until you consider the lost humanity that such a view of the workplace entails. If the organization is a machine and employees nothing more than parts of the machine, emotions are irrelevant. So are individual life circumstances. So are employee ideas and insights that could lead to organizational breakthroughs and refreshing winds of innovation and change.

An organization that focuses on processes at the expense of people may well be highly efficient, especially at completing repetitive, simple tasks. But such an organization is prone to bullying because the inherent value and dignity of human beings is overlooked. It's easy to step on people if their humanity is merely a liability, if they are seen as especially complicated and unruly parts of the machine.

Ironically, leaders who focus on processes at the expense of people pursue the goal of increased productivity at all costs yet pay no attention to "the human side of doing business," which in fact enhances productivity rather than detracting from it. They fail to realize this fact: Only when the precious humanity of employees is upheld can maximum levels of productivity be achieved.

Rules Before Creativity

This leads to the third characteristic of bully-prone organizations: a preoccupation with rules at the expense of creativity and innovation. Rules are necessary but when they dominate an organization to the point of squelching creativity (ideas and insights that can lead to organizational breakthroughs and innovation), the organization suffers.

When rules become dominant to this extent, the workplace feels sterile and employee zest for work is reduced. Employees lose engagement in work and are less likely to take pride in what they do. A sense of teamwork has no chance to gel because employee initiative, whether individual or group, is not encouraged.

An organization that puts rules before creativity is prone to bullying because it kills pleasure in work. In the "creativity vacuum" that a rules-fixated environment creates, human beings become bitter and defeatist. Lacking a vision to fulfill, a team to which they can belong, a chance to contribute to something bigger than themselves, they regress rather than grow. Hurt dominates. Mistrust festers. Negative attitudes and behaviors multiply. A prevailing ambiance of goodwill, which goes a long way toward making work bearable and even enjoyable, is gone.

Over time, a rules-bound organization dies a slow death and so do the employees—especially the most talented and creative among them, who want to share their knowledge and insights, who want to contribute to their full potential, but cannot. Forced to the sidelines, these employees may be labeled as "nonconformist" and admonished for lack of team play.

Unable to bear the suffocation, some leave the organization. Others stay to collect a paycheck but mentally "check out" from work. Having tried over and over again to present new ideas and possibilities, and each time, having been shut down for violating the rules— often unwritten rules about what is or isn't allowed in the organization—they are there but not there. They do just enough to stay out of trouble and keep their jobs but their sparkle is gone, the full extent of their talent no longer in view.

Bully-prone versus Bully-free

A term I often use to capture all three of these characteristics is "bureaucratic"—not because bullying organizations are necessarily office-based, but rather that they lack flexibility and the collaborative spirit that is a key prerequisite for business success.

The opposite of a bureaucratic organization is an organic organization. Healthy and life-giving on many levels, an organic organization welcomes employee input and encourages employees to become involved in decision-making. The decentralized authority structure of such an organization helps to ensure that employees are empowered and engaged. Bullying is rare.

An organic organization values human beings, understanding that processes improve when the value of people is upheld. An organic organization is flexible, refusing to let rules supersede the importance of fresh thinking, which sometimes requires rules to change.

Fortunately, organizations can change from bureaucratic to organic, from 'bully-prone' to 'bully-free' if they so desire. Will transformation happen quickly or easily? No, but each step forward is worth celebrating and over time, it's amazing what concerted efforts can achieve.

The Tragedy of Bullying from a Human— and Business—Point of View

Where would you rather work? In a bully-free, organic organization or a bully-prone, bureaucratic one? A second question: Which of the two organizations would you vote most likely to succeed?

If you chose the bully-free, organic organization in each case, you've demonstrated a simple fact: what is best and healthiest for people in the workplace is also likely to make sense from a business point of view. Conversely, what is undesirable for people is also bad business. Leaders who harass or support bullying may believe they are engaging in necessary measures to manage and control employees, squeezing out the most from them. In reality they are taking a shotgun to the heart and soul of the organization and leading it to its demise.

I remember my first day on the job at a bully-prone, bureaucratic organization. My boss told me we had to "ride the employees here" so they'd produce more. I witnessed him screaming at employees he thought were slowing the assembly line. He stood over others and watched their every move, staring with disdain.

He was like a pit-bull, clenching mistrust and hostility in his teeth.

The necessity of negativity was like a religion for him. It was almost as if he found virtue in practicing abuse. When I declined to "ride the employees" as instructed, it was as if I'd betrayed both him and the organization. I stood my ground on this decision as time went by, refusing to practice anything but leadership methods that upheld the dignity and value of human beings. Even when the employees I supervised achieved significantly higher levels of productivity than they had while being mistreated, I was not forgiven for the heresy of failing to conform.

More and more, as mentioned in Part I of this book, I saw the writing on the wall. I saw that I couldn't last at the organization, and that the organization itself couldn't last. Today, this organization as well as its bully-prone competitor, where I also worked, have either filed for bankruptcy or are on the verge of filing for bankruptcy. Both organizations are laying off thousands of employees, closing plants and seeking government assistance to survive.

If only they'd listened to the "nonconformists" instead of ignoring or punishing them. If only they'd taken steps to become healthier while there was still time.

CHAPTER 12

Getting Down to Business: What to Do If You're Being Bullied

The truth is, you have more power and strength inside you than you might realize.

"It's hopeless."
"There's no way out."
"Nothing I do makes a difference."
"I'm stuck with it."
"It's out of my control."

If you've had such thoughts, as a person suffering bullying in the workplace, you're not alone. The situation can indeed seem overwhelming. The cumulative effects can be severe. Tragically, it is no surprise that people succumb to hopelessness and despair under the ongoing pressures of harassment on the job.

Change Your Mindset

As you know, I, too, have been bullied at work. Because of this I've earned the right to speak a difficult truth: if you feel powerless to stop the harassment, you are giving in to passivity. You have adopted a position of "learned helplessness" in relation to the abuse.

As previously mentioned, learned helplessness is a psychological condition in which a person has learned to believe that he or she has no control over the hurtful situation; and furthermore, that any effort to try and change it will be futile. Shackled by a fatalistic, "why-even-try?" mentality, such a person not only feels helpless but also hopeless. He or she sees only the darkness, not the light.

If this describes you, know that learned helplessness is not your only option, as much as it might seem to be. It is not helping you. Figuratively speaking, it is allowing someone to shoot or stab you again and again, with neither protest nor resistance on your part.

Difficult words, yes. You may feel I'm blaming you for the continuation of the abuse. You may feel I don't understand how bad your situation is. But set your reservations aside for a moment, and hear the good news: *You can choose to change the belief that you are helpless.* Just as helplessness is learned, so is hopefulness. Changing your mindset from one of learned helplessness to one of *learned hopefulness* is the first step you must take in dealing with the abuse.

Am I blaming you for the continuation of the abuse? Absolutely not! Nor am I suggesting that learning to change your mindset will be easy. The worse your situation is and the longer it has lasted, the greater your challenge will be. But the fact remains that changing your mindset is your only hope. It's the only way to say "yes" to yourself, to healing, to life.

"But how do I change?" you might ask. "How do I stop believing I'm helpless? How do I learn to hope?" Good questions. I will answer them by imagining you are sitting right here beside me. Here's what I'd say if you asked me these questions as someone I was mentoring, or as a family member or friend.

"You must start by believing in yourself," I'd say. "You must make the choice to begin believing in yourself and loving yourself enough to stop buying into the helplessness lie. The truth is, you can help yourself, scary as it might seem. The truth is, you have more power and strength inside you than you might realize. One more thing: you must reach out for help like never before. You will not be able to walk this path alone."

Lay the Groundwork

Adopting a mental attitude of *learned hopefulness* is a choice you'll need to make again and again, each time negative thoughts return. The more you practice learned hopefulness and let its truths sink into you, the more effectively you'll be able to deal with the harassment. Little by little, you'll become stronger mentally, allowing you to take the practical steps you need to take. Remember to read and re-read this affirmation often *"I am loved. I matter. I will not be defeated. I will be victorious. I will survive this situation. I will not let anyone steal my hope.*"

What to Do Right Now If You are Being Bullied

Document

The first practical step is one many people overlook: Document, document, document. Each and every time you are bullied at work, put the details on paper. Do this as soon as possible after the incident.

The more documentation you have, the better. The more details you provide, the better. As a minimum, cover these points:

- What is the current date and time?
- What was the date and time of the incident?
- Where did it occur?
- Who was involved in the situation?
- Who witnessed it?
- What did the bully say or do?
- Recreate the scene, offering as many facts as you can. Also tell someone about the incident immediately after it occurs. Don't keep it secret! You have nothing to hide. Allow the facts to see the light of day.

Seek External Assistance

A strong support network is critical to help you deal with the harassment and maintain hope. You need friends and family to listen to you, support and encourage you. You also need professional support. Don't be afraid or hesitate to seek professional help. If you've never sought help from a counselor or psychologist, this is the time. You'll gain more from counseling than you might expect: support, yes, but also an objective caring perspective on what is happening to you, how it is affecting you and what you can do to take control of your life.

Pay close attention to your mental, emotional and physical state. If you notice changes, such as crying spells, difficulty sleeping, or other indicators of depression or stress, take them as cues to get professional help. Perhaps you'll decide to call the counselor or psychologist a friend or co-worker has recommended. Perhaps you'll schedule an appointment with your family physician. Perhaps you'll meet with the spiritual leader at your place of worship.

Whomever you consult, know you're doing the right thing by reaching out. You're living through an extraordinarily difficult period in your life. The pressures are intense. By reaching out for professional help, you're taking responsibility for your own health and showing respect for yourself. You're equipping yourself to deal with the bully. Later, should you decide to pursue legal action (more on that later) your treatment from a counselor, psychologist or physician will help support the claim that bullying indeed caused the stress or other ailment you suffered.

Confront the Bully

Once you've adopted an attitude of learned hopefulness, are documenting all incidents of bullying and have created a strong support network, you'll be in a good position to confront the person who is harassing you.

Here is where things might start to get scary for you. "Confront *him*? Confront *her*? Are you crazy?" I can almost hear you say the words.

I, too, was terrified by the prospect of confrontation but here's what I learned: if you properly equip yourself, standing up to your bully is not as intimidating as you might expect. You'll need to have your facts on paper. You'll need to have your support people in place. And you'll need a plan. In essence, your mission is to convey to the bully that you will not tolerate the offensive behavior and it **must stop**.

Each situation is unique. But as a rule, I recommend confronting the bully as soon as possible after the incident, each and every time an incident occurs. If the incident occurs during the day, you might want to document it that night and confront the bully the following day. You'll want to confront the bully in private, perhaps in his or her office, for the sake of confidentiality. If possible, bring in a third party to act as a witness and support person for you. Or ask to set up a meeting with your human resources (HR) department, if you prefer.

Go into the situation knowing you're likely to meet with resistance, but with the confidence that comes from knowing you're in control and doing the right thing. Speak with confidence and authority even though you may be feeling uncertain and scared inside. When the bully responds in a negative way, whether by getting angry, threatening to fire you or issuing some other threat, stand your ground. Let him or her know you won't be intimidated.

If you have yet to involve HR, this is the time to let the bully know you're planning to report the offensive behavior to HR—and your manager and supervisor, if you have yet to involve either of these parties. If the bully is your manager or supervisor, report the behavior to his or her boss and to HR.

Sharing this information may well trigger additional hostility on the bully's part. Stay calm. If you know what to expect, you've documented all the facts and you've got a strong support network in place, (perhaps including one supporter right beside you), you'll find that staying calm under pressure is indeed possible for you.

File a Formal Complaint

Once you've confronted the bully and notified all appropriate parties within the company, wait to see if the behavior changes. If it doesn't, follow your company's procedures to file a formal complaint with HR. Please note that organizations do not have an anti-bullying policy, but they do have policies in place regarding other harassments such as sexual or racial harassment. Use those policies as a guide for filing your complaint.

HR representatives should respond by conducting a formal investigation and helping to rectify the situation.

It is fulfilling their responsibility to ensure the workplace is healthy and safe for everyone.

A word of caution: On paper, HR is there to support you. In reality, it may hurt you more than help you. If bullying is systemic within the company, as it often is, HR representatives will find it easier to get rid of one person (you) than to deal with the larger and far thornier problem of company-wide harassment and negativity. Don't be surprised if HR treats you like the perpetrator, not the victim, even if you've followed all of the proper channels in presenting your concerns.

Consult a Lawyer

What should you do if, after taking all of these steps, the situation doesn't change? What if it worsens? Here's my advice: Talk to a lawyer about the emotional distress you're suffering because of your hostile work environment. If you belong to one or more protected groups, you may want to determine if you're being bullied because of your status in one or more of those categories. If you are, find out what your legal options are.

Because bullying legislation has yet to be passed in the U.S. and in most provinces of Canada (more on this in the following chapter) you'll have difficulty convincing a judge to rule in your favor. However, it may still be in your best interest to prove that you suffered personal injury as a result of emotional distress caused by the bully who is a representative of your organization.

You'll have to provide documentation of the bullying, as well as proof that you received treatment from healthcare providers as a result of the harassment. Most organizations will want to settle the matter through mediation or other means rather than having their "dirty laundry" exposed. They'll want the targeted person to go away, not the bully.

Do It for *You*

In taking these steps, you are sending a clear message to the bully, your colleagues, your bosses and the organization as a whole. You are saying that you respect yourself. You are saying that you value yourself too much to allow the bullying to continue. You are standing strong in order to uphold your vision of what a healthy workplace should be.

The journey toward regaining control of your life and eliminating the bullying can be long and frustrating. It was for me. But if you persevere, you'll find as I did that the outcome is well worth the struggle. You'll become a stronger person. You'll realize how courageous and resilient you are. You'll gain new insights about yourself and discover new opportunities.

Remember, you are taking this journey for you and no one else. Remember, too, that if you don't stand up for yourself, no one else will. Move forward with confidence. Know that the future holds many possibilities for you. Reach out and grab them. You are worth it!

CHAPTER 13

Life After Bullying: My Emerging Role as a Healthy Workplace Lobbyist

In New York State and elsewhere in North America we are on the verge of a breakthrough in seeing anti-psychological harassment legislation passed.

I don't know what life will hold for you once your bullying experience is past. But I do know that light always dawns. I hope that part of your healing will be to help others by sharing what you've learned from your ordeal.

I hope that you will want to take a stand against workplace bullying. I hope that you will want to fight for justice and truth. These have been my desires, since healing from the bullying I experienced. My trauma is receding into memory but my passion for fighting workplace injustice grows stronger each day.

A Lobbyist is Born

During the early stages of my research into workplace bullying, I was surprised to learn, as mentioned previously, that the U.S. has no laws addressing workplace bullying. In Canada, only Quebec has legislation in place. Although Ontario has amended its Occupational Health and Safety Act to address violence and harassment in the workplace, these amendments do not specifically target workplace bullying.

The conspicuous failure of lawmakers to adequately address workplace bullying has helped me a great deal. Even before recognizing this significant and unacceptable gap in the law, I was inclined to take action. Now I knew exactly where to channel my efforts. And there was no time to waste!

Fortunately, as part of my research, I discovered New York Healthy Workplace Advocates, an organization whose name brought to mind the title of my previous book, *Hope For A Healthy Workplace*. After coming across the organization's website (www.nyhwa.org) I spoke by telephone with one of its state coordinators. I knew I had to get involved.

New York Healthy Workplace Advocates consists of citizen lobbyists seeking to introduce, support and pass legislation that addresses bullying on the job. The fit is perfect for me. I'm excited to be a member of this group. These people have had similar experiences with workplace bullying and are willing to take a stand, as I am.

At the Frontlines

My first lobbying assignment with New York Healthy Workplace Advocates took place on January 26, 2009. As I wrote in my journal:

> I'm sitting in a dingy hotel room in Albany, N.Y., having driven here last night from Buffalo to meet with the team. As I made my way down the New York State Thruway, I encountered falling snow and snow-covered roads from Buffalo to Rochester. I wondered if my entire trip would consist of snowy roads and limited visibility. Although I thought about turning around a few times, I decided to continue. Eventually, the snow stopped, the roads turned dry and the sun broke through the clouds. I knew in my spirit I was meant to continue on this journey.

> I arrived at the hotel at 8 p.m. After checking in and having a bite to eat, I contacted my colleagues who were in another room assembling packets. I felt as if I were back in the 1960s. The room where my colleagues were working had a '60s feel. I sensed that I'd entered into an adventure that would forever change my life. Packets, papers, labels and other materials were strewn on the bed, chairs, tables and wherever else there was space.

> Tom and Mike had already begun assembling packets of material they'd photocopied: flyers as well as research information on workplace bullying and its effects on employers and employees. I took my coat off and jumped right in. As we assembled packets, we talked about the challenges ahead in making

contact with government representatives and raising public awareness of healthy workplace issues. Tom and Mike, both experienced lobbyists, were eager to share their insights.

I soaked in as much information as I could and knew in my heart that this is exactly where I needed to be. Excitement welled up inside me as I thought about what could happen if the Healthy Workplace Bill were to pass. Had civil rights activists during the 1960s felt anything like this? Oh, to be part of something bigger than myself, just as they had been.

The next morning, the team met at the Capitol Building cafeteria to discuss plans for the day. We received our assignments to lobby for the Healthy Workplace Bill for 30 minutes each with various Senate and Assembly representatives. During the first couple of meetings, I mainly watched and listened carefully. After the second meeting, I took the lead. How exciting to be part of the action! My passion for the cause grew with each meeting I attended that day.

Due to other commitments, I left Albany the next afternoon while the rest of the team stayed on to continue the work. I've since returned to Albany to lobby and have written letters to government representatives in support of the bill. In the future, I intend to solicit union support and request media coverage on the need for anti-psychological harassment legislation.

Coming Full Circle

Only one week prior to my lobbying debut in Albany, I'd travelled 10 hours overnight by bus to attend the inauguration of Barack Obama as the first black president of the U.S. I'd walked the streets of Washington, D.C., with millions of others, floating on the powerful wave of celebration that was in the air.

In Albany, as in Washington, I was reminded of what a difference one person can make—and what the combined efforts of many can achieve. In Albany, as in Washington, a sense of history-in-the-making overwhelmed me, fueling my desire to do my part.

Both events brought to mind an experience of many years earlier, when I visited Albany on a class trip in 8th grade. Going back in time to recreate those memories:

> *I am 12 years old. After years of hearing about the struggles and victories of the civil rights movement, I'm finally here—at the Capitol Building in Albany. As the bus pulls up to the entrance, the building takes my breath away. It looks like a palace: grand and majestic, unlike any building I've ever seen.*
>
> *The tour guide meets us inside the lobby and starts talking about the history of the building. I listen with interest but I'm impatient, I want to get to the Assembly and Senate chambers where all of the big decisions are made. My classmates and I stand in awe as my teacher begins talking once again, just as she has in class, about how bills and then laws are passed.*
>
> *All around us, grownups in dark suits are talking and walking as if very important things are going on. I know they're involved in something big, something too big for me to understand, but something I want to be part of some day.*

As a result of the class trip to Albany, I decided to become a lawyer and eventually a politician so I could help pass laws. Years later, I attended but never finished law school, having found that law was not my calling after all. Still, how apt it felt, years later, to return to Albany as a lobbyist. Although I'm not directly involved in passing laws, I have the power to influence those who do. I fully intend to use that power to help get the Healthy Workplace Bill passed.

Update from New York State

When the Healthy Workplace Bill becomes law it will make history as the first legislation of its kind in the U.S. and one of the only laws of its kind in North America. In New York State, bullies and organizations that allow workplace bullying would finally be held liable for the damages they inflict.

According to the New York Healthy Workplace Advocates' website, the bill

> "...extends protection to all employees, working for either public or private employers, regardless of protected group status, who seek redress for being subjected to an abusive work environment. It becomes unlawful [under the provisions of the bill] to be subjected to another employee whose malicious conduct sabotages or undermines the targeted person's work performance."

At the time of this writing, the New York State Assembly has passed the Healthy Workplace study bill but a Republican/Democrat stalemate is delaying passage of the companion bill in the Senate. We remain hopeful, considering this only a minor setback. The New York State Public Employees Federation, which represents 59,000 professional, scientific and technical employees, supports this legislation. Similarly, The NAACP (National Association for the Advancement of Colored People) a civil rights organization for ethnic minorities in the U.S., has resolved to seek legislation that would deem workplace bullying illegal. With success in sight, we press on in the work of spreading the word about workplace bullying and influencing our lawmakers. Visit www.bulliednomore.com for updates.

Future Outlook

Fortunately, although history offers little precedent for the kind of legislation we have in mind, public opinion is on our side. As the public becomes aware of the destructive impact of workplace bullying on individuals, organizations and entire economies, voters want healthy workplace legislation passed.

In recent research I conducted within New York State, a full 90% of respondents said the state needs workplace bullying laws. Even more—93%—said employers should establish anti-psychological harassment policies similar to existing anti-discrimination and anti-sexual harassment policies.

In related findings:
- 71% of respondents indicated they'd either been bullied at work or knew someone who had been.
- 75% indicated they'd witnessed others being bullied.

What You Can Do

Only you can determine what your next step will be. You can allow your pain to hold you captive or break free and make a difference in the lives of others. I chose the latter.

I will continue to conduct research in this field and use my speaking and writing to share my message with audiences throughout the U.S. and Canada. I will do my part to help eliminate bullying in the workplace. What can you do?

Here are some ideas:
- Ask the leaders in your organization to create a healthy workplace policy.
- Urge lawmakers within your state or province to establish anti-psychological harassment legislation.
- If you see injustice occurring at work, speak up. Don't become part of the problem by ignoring it.
- Reach out and become a friend to the person who is being tormented.

- If you notice that a co-worker's behavior or attitude has changed, ask him or her if everything is ok. Show you care by getting involved.
- Make sure your behavior doesn't contribute to emotional abuse that is already taking place.
- Lead by example and treat everyone with respect.
- Stand up to the bully on behalf of the person who is suffering.
- It bears repeating: Reach out. Be a friend.

Closing Thoughts

In New York State and elsewhere in North America we are on the verge of a breakthrough in seeing anti-psychological harassment legislation passed. When New York State passes the Healthy Workplace Bill, it will assume a proud place in history as the first state government to do so.

Slavery was once the norm. Now it has virtually disappeared, having been recognized by most of us as barbaric and unjust.

Beating your wife and children was once considered a 'family affair'. Now it has been outlawed as a violent and abusive practice.

The same turnaround is before us with workplace bullying. If you do what you can to fight it, you, too, can take pride in knowing you've done your part. Along the way, your life will be enriched in ways you can't fully imagine, just as mine has been.

CHAPTER 14

The Ultimate Price of Bullying: Why I Won't Stop Fighting Workplace Abuse

Carry yourself with confidence,
knowing that you are someone to be
valued, respected and loved.

Jodie Zebell had a horrible pain in her stomach. She felt so sick and weary she didn't feel that she could face her supervisor again. After several months of being bullied by her supervisor and numerous failed attempts to change jobs, she decided to resign.

The human resources official whom she submitted her resignation to asked her to take the weekend to reconsider. He also asked her to document each incident of bullying that had taken place.

Days later, on Sunday, Feb. 3, 2008, Jodie made a decision that would send shock waves through her family. Wracked with anxiety and unable to think clearly—unable

to consider the full impact on her loved ones or imagine better days ahead—she took her own life, leaving her husband
and two young children bereft.

She was 31 years old, with a promising future ahead of
her. A future she forfeited because workplace bullying had
put a veil of darkness on her soul.

Today, her aunt Joie Bostwick tells Jodie's story in order
to raise awareness of workplace bullying. Jodie's voice is
forever silenced. But Joie, despite the freshness of her
wounds, speaks out on her behalf. Joie wants people to know
the terrible impact of workplace bullying. She wants other
families to be spared the suffering her family has borne.

In Memory of Jodie

I am celebrating my birthday as I write these words.
I am grateful to be alive and to have reached this mile-
stone as an author, with one more book about to make
its way into the world. But I am sad for Jodie and her
family. I tell you Jodie's story not to sensationalize the
issue of workplace bullying but to show you just how
devastating it can be.

Jodie's story is fact, not fiction. She was employed as
a mammographer in Wisconsin. Her aunt, Joie, of
Naples, Florida, told me Jodie's story while we were
both in Albany, New York lobbying for anti-bullying
legislation.

In a photograph, Jodie's beautiful smile and girlish
pixie haircut make it seem unlikely that she could be
lost to us. Such a fresh-faced young mom, with two

little ones eager for her smile, her hugs, and her love. How can such a tragedy happen?

Jodie had hopes and dreams that were just as real as yours and mine. She wanted to get an education. To be happy in her work. To raise a family. To live a good life. The day after graduating from high school in Florida, Jodie moved to Wisconsin to live with her dad. She attended technical college, then moved on to complete her studies at the University of Wisconsin School of Radiologic Technology.

In 1997, Jodie met her future husband Scott. The following year, she graduated from the University of Wisconsin and began working as an X-ray technologist. As she wrote in her blog: "I miss the warm Florida weather and hope to become a resident of the Sunshine state once again."

Speaking Out for Jodie … and for YOU

Just like her aunt, I, too, want to be a voice for Jodie. And not only for her, but for all the other people who have taken their lives because they couldn't bear the thought of being bullied one more day.

Just as passionately, I want to be the voice of employees who suffer in silence, hoping that someday the bullying will stop.

I want to be the voice of employees who are healing and trying to figure out what to do next.

I want to be the voice that says to lawmakers, "Enough is enough."

I wrote this book to bring hope to bullied individuals, their families and loved ones.

I wrote this book to shed light on the ever-growing problem of workplace bullying and the staggering toll it takes.

I wrote this book for the mother who contacted me and told me she was going to commit suicide.

For Tracey, who is now homeless as a result of her bullying experience.

For Jill, who had to quit her job because her bosses bullied her for being overweight.

For Tom, Mike, Ken, Mary and others whose lives have been turned upside down by bullies.

For YOU.

For the rest of my life, I will fight bullying in the workplace because I care about you too much to stop.

Perspective on Your Journey

Throughout this book, I've provided insights gleaned from experience and research—insights I believe will help you on your journey. I want to remind you that your bullying experience will only last for a season. Eventually, the season will change just as winter turns to spring, spring gives way to summer and so on.

The secret in life, as in farming, is to embrace the current season and to prepare for the next.

If you're beginning to experience behavior you suspect is bullying, then you have the opportunity to nip it in the bud right away.

If you've been bullied for some time and are ready for it to end, then you must begin to create an escape plan.

Or you may have removed yourself from the bullying situation and now are going through the healing season.

Wherever you are on your journey, be patient with yourself. Think of farmers who patiently wait for their crops to grow. They tend to the land and nurture it, knowing that harvest time lies ahead.

Once you've gone through your healing season, you, too, will reap the benefits. You'll discover many new and exciting things about yourself. You'll come to value yourself and others more. You'll have the courage and strength to venture into new realms and embrace your life with open arms. You'll pursue your life's purpose with great determination and passion.

One day you'll look back on your bullying experience and appreciate it for molding you into the person you've become.

Light for Your Path

I'm excited about what the future holds for you, just as I am about what it holds for me. I've grown a lot as a result of my workplace bullying experience. I appreciate life more and don't take anything for granted. I've been blessed and know that blessings are waiting for you as well.

My dear friend, I encourage you to cling to hope, knowing you will find a way to escape the bullying.

I encourage you to love yourself, muster up the courage to change your situation and say "No!" to the abuse.

I encourage you to remove the shackles of helplessness that have bound you and replace them with the sense of freedom that hope instills.

Continue to believe in yourself and uphold your own worth. Carry yourself with confidence, knowing that you are someone to be valued, respected and loved.

Finally, do your part to eradicate workplace bullying. Only you know what you can do to support this cause.

May God richly bless you and heal your life.

TO CONTACT THE AUTHOR:

LISA M. S. BARROW, DM
3806 Union Rd., Unit #107
Cheektowaga, New York 14225
716-238-1298
drlisabarrow@gmail.com
www.bulliednomore.com